W9-BUH-865

Brunswick County Library
109 W Moore Street
Southport, NC 28461

WITHDRAWN

A PRACTICAL HANDBOOK OF
ARCHAEOLOGY

Hickmans

A PRACTICAL HANDBOOK OF
ARCHAEOLOGY
A Beginner's Guide to Unearthing the Past

An invaluable tool for amateur archaeologists with 300 step-by-step photographs, maps and illustrations from excavations around the world

Christopher Catling

Consultant: Fiona Haughey

HERMES
HOUSE

Brunswick County Library
109 W Moore Street
Southport, NC 28461

This edition is published by Hermes House, an imprint of Anness Publishing Ltd, 108 Great Russell Street, London WC1B 3NA; info@anness.com

www.hermeshouse.com; www.annesspublishing.com

If you like the images in this book and would like to investigate using them for publishing, promotions or advertising, please visit our website www.practicalpictures.com for more information.

© Anness Publishing Ltd 2014

All rights reserved. No part of this publication may be reproduced, stored in a retrieval system, or transmitted in any way or by any means, electronic, mechanical, photocopying, recording or otherwise, without the prior written permission of the copyright holder.

A CIP catalogue record for this book is available from the British Library.

Publisher: Joanna Lorenz
Editorial Director: Helen Sudell
Project Editor: Melanie Hibbert
Production Controller: Pirong Wang
Photographers: Robert Pickett and Mark Wood
Picture Research: Louise Cooper and Zoë Hughes Gough
Book Design: Ian Sandom
Cover Design: Balley Design

Previously published as part of a larger volume, *Archaeology Step-By-Step*

PUBLISHER'S NOTE
Although the advice and information in this book are believed to be accurate and true at the time of going to press, neither the authors nor the publisher can accept any legal responsiblity or liability for any errors or omissions that may have been made, nor for any inaccuracies nor for any loss, harm or injury that comes about from following instructions or advice in this book.

CONTENTS

Introduction

Some people become so obsessed with ancient pots, bones and standing stones that they devote their lives to archaeology. They are motivated by the challenge of trying to deduce from the scant remains found at many excavations how our ancestors lived and what they thought and believed.

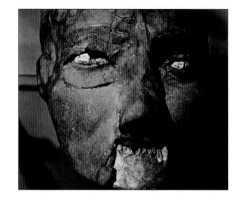

Above Human skulls preserved in plaster were recovered from the West Bank, Middle East, where they were buried some 7,000 years ago. Archaeologists will ask what part they played in ancient belief and ancestor worship.

Archaeologists are not driven by money. While they are not treasure hunters, there isn't an archaeologist alive whose pulse would not quicken at the sight of a beautiful brooch emerging from the soil. However, an archaeologist would not ask 'how much is it worth?', but 'how old is it, why is it here and what can we learn about the maker and the owner?'

Archaeology is rooted in curiosity rather than dreams of wealth, and anybody can be an archaeologist – it isn't necessary to have a university degree or a special licence. If you have ever wondered 'how old is my house, how did the previous inhabitants use the rooms and what did the rooms used to look like?', you are already asking some archaeological questions.

Riddle solvers

Being interested in the past can be frustrating because the record is so incomplete. Materials tend to survive only if they are durable, such as stone or pottery, or if special conditions prevail, such as permafrost (which acts like a deep freeze to preserve organic remains) or extreme aridity, (where the air is too dry for the survival of microbes that cause wood, paper, grass, cloth or hair to rot). That is why archaeologists have devised more and more ingenious ways to extract information and

meaning from the detritus and accidental survivals of the past. Being unashamed scavengers, archaeologists are also willing to borrow ideas from other disciplines. They have raided the tool chests of historians and linguists, soil scientists and geologists, botanists and anatomists, anthropologists and geographers, and art and architectural historians. More recently, huge strides in archaeological knowledge have been achieved by using scientific and medical

technologies – carbon-14 dating, CAT scanning or DNA analysis – as tools for dating the past, looking inside mummified human remains or tracing the genetic origins of people, animals and food plants.

A winning occupation

All these factors help to answer the question of why archaeology is so fascinating: it combines intellectual stimulation with physical exercise, it is an integrative subject that draws on many other disciplines, it is a subject that touches on all our lives and asks questions about human origins and development, and it leads to a deeper understanding of the world in which we live.

There is plenty of pleasure and knowledge to be gained from taking part in archaeology, and this book will achieve its aim if it shows you how easy it is to turn from an armchair archaeologist, watching other people doing archaeology on television, into an active archaeologist doing your own research.

Above Archaeologists can provide dates for ancient ceramics, like this Chinese Ming dynasty vase (1367–1644), by studying glazing techniques and manufacturing methods.

Right The temple of Tholos at Delphi, Greece (380–360BC). Such complete monuments are rare – more often, archaeologists have to work with fragments of past lives.

Above What all archaeologists have in common is that they study the physical remains of the human past, from whole landscapes to microscopic objects, or the symbols left by previous peoples, such as this Aboriginal cave art at Bungle Bungle, Western Australia.

What is archaeology?

There are numerous definitions of archaeology: so many that some people talk about 'archaeologies' in the plural. Some argue that archaeology is a way of thinking, a creative process, others say it is a set of questions about the past, while some define it as the study of human experience – how people have lived in the past and responded to their environment.

There are also many different kinds of archaeologist: some that dig and some that study the results of other people's digs; archaeologists that specialize in a period, a culture, a region or a type of artefact – flint tools or Roman coins, for example. There are landscape archaeologists, terrestrial archaeologists and marine archaeologists (there are no extraterrestrial archaeologists yet, though NASA does employ an archaeologist to study satellite images!).

Archaeology versus history

Historians also study the past, but they do so by using written and oral records. Archaeologists can delve deeper into the past to study the thousands of years of human endeavour that occurred before written or oral records began. Archaeology can also supplement history by looking for material evidence that doesn't appear in the historical record.

For example, history tells us that Shakespeare's plays were performed at London's Rose Theatre. Only by excavating the theatre have we been able to reconstruct its original appearance. Finds from the theatre site, such as bottles, fruit remains, nutshells, shellfish and tobacco pipes, tell us that the audience smoked, drank and chomped their way through snacks throughout the performances – facts that add a human element to the historical record.

What Do Archaeologists Really Do?

The popular image of the archaeologist is of an intrepid hole digger looking for buried treasure, probably dressed in eccentric clothes. Though there are some archaeologists that cultivate this image, there are many archaeologists who wear suits to work and might never have held a trowel in their lives.

Above The ethical treatment of human remains is an important part of responsible excavation.

There are archaeologists in a surprising number of fields: they work in the media, in schools, in parliaments and the civil service, in museums, engineering, publishing and the travel and tourism industries. Some run large public companies or institutions (for example, the UK's Big Lottery Fund); others are employed by the army, the police and the secret services. Yet others have a day job as a banker or farmer, and turn to archaeology as a weekend hobby. There are even rock star archaeologists (former Rolling Stones guitarist Bill Wyman has published archaeology books, as has singer Julian Cope, while ex-Beatle Sir Paul McCartney sponsors the UK's annual Conservation Awards).

Training for life

It is archaeology's proud boast that it is democratic, classless and integrative, and that the skills involved in archaeology are the ones that make for a successful career in many walks of life – these skills include team building, problem solving, communication, empirical observation and deduction, and human resource management.

There are also many different fields in which to specialize, from field archaeologists, who do actually dig holes, to those who master the skills of blacksmithing to understand the techniques used by Roman armourers, or those who devote their lives to identifying the diseases of past populations through bone remains.

This book shows how 'practical archaeology' is a process of many stages, from data gathering and initial field survey to taking a decision to dig (or not to dig), analysing finds, reporting the results, pinning down dates, conducting specialized research and reporting the results. Throughout the book, we will continually encounter two main approaches to fieldwork: research archaeology, where the aim is to find answers for specific questions, and rescue archaeology, where the digger makes a record of archaeology being threatened by development or some other destructive force, such as coastal erosion. It is therefore worth looking at both in greater detail here.

Research archaeology

Whether amateur or professional, student or professor, research archaeologists can select and define their own field of study, choose their own sites to investigate and frame their own set of questions. These might be as simple as 'what can I find out about the lives of the people that have lived on this plot of land in the past?' or they can be as complex as 'what do the features of this landscape tell us about the religious practice and beliefs of our ancestors?'

Research might focus on a site as small as a single house plot or garden, or a whole town, or on a landscape that might range in scale from a village to a whole river system of hundreds of miles. Alternatively, the aim might be

Above Rescue excavations often take place on development sites where their trowelling contrasts with earth-moving on a huge scale.

Above Archaeologists often study traditional crafts such as blacksmithing to understand the development of ancient industry.

Above Thanks to television programmes that feature 'live digs', many of us are now more familiar with what archaeologists do.

to study a particular type of monument, such as rock art, burial mounds, shrines or medieval gardens, or to tackle complex thematic questions, examining religion, the countryside, industry, trade, transport, diet or cultural change.

Rescue archaeology

By contrast, rescue archaeology involves salvaging information before it is destroyed. In some parts of the world it is impossible to put a spade into the ground without stumbling upon archaeological remains. It isn't practical to preserve all the archaeology – to attempt to do so would freeze development in just about every major city in the world.

Instead, rescue archaeologists work with developers who build new roads, houses, factories, pipelines, schools or hospitals. In many countries planning laws require developers to consult experts and assess the likely impact of the development on the environment – both on the natural environment, with its delicate ecosystems, and on the historic environment, consisting of

Above Students often volunteer at excavations as part of a further education course.

existing historic buildings and buried remains. Highly skilled rescue archaeologists work in an environment more akin to that of a consultant architect, builder, surveyor or engineer. Their task is to make an objective assessment of the importance of the archaeological remains, deciding what can be sacrificed to the development and when it is necessary to carry

Opportunities for volunteers

The techniques that are used in research archaeology and rescue archaeology are largely identical, but the working conditions can be different. Volunteers are rarely allowed to take part in rescue archaeology because of the training and experience required to work on building sites – where there are often numerous hazards – and archaeologists often need to work against the clock. The archaeologists are contractually obliged to complete their work within a set period of days to avoid holding up the development.

Research-led excavations are often conducted at a slower pace over several years by university archaeology departments or a local archaeology society. Many are run as community digs, perhaps organized by the local museum, or as training excavations for university archaeology students and anyone else who is interested. You are usually expected to stay for at least a week, and you may have to pay a small fee to cover the costs of training, food and accommodation.

out an excavation to 'rescue' what will otherwise be lost.

Put crudely, archaeology is viewed by many developers as a 'contaminant' that has to be removed before the site can legally be developed. However, for the rescue archaeologist, removing that contaminant is a lucky-dip activity. They don't get to choose, but have to tackle whatever comes up.

INVESTIGATING THE PAST WITHOUT DIGGING

One of the ironies of archaeology is that it destroys the material on which it depends. Digging a site, no matter how painstakingly it is done, involves removing soil and the materials within it for examination. Once this is done, the site can never be returned to its original state: the stratigraphy, which is vital for dating the remains, will have been irrevocably disturbed. Instead, the excavator's records of what they found is all that is left.

So, contrary to the popular belief, digging is not the defining activity of archaeology. Any digging is preceded by a huge amount of information gathering. This includes studying historical maps and noting the changes over time, analysing placenames for clues to past uses, assessing patterns in the landscape, especially as seen from the air, and compiling any other archive information about a site.

Opposite The dusting of snow in this aerial view of Stonehenge highlights some of the less obvious features.

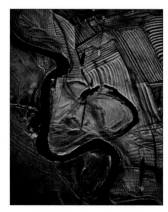

Above This aerial photograph of the River Dove taken in Uttoxeter, central England, shows a buried lake and ancient ploughmarks.

Above Research into the previous history of a site is being made easier by the increasing amount of data accessible on the internet.

Above These ship-shaped stone settings at Anundshög, Sweden, offer visible evidence of medieval burial practice.

Non-invasive Archaeology

Archaeology is never about leaping in and digging at random, just to see what might be there. Instead, all archaeology begins by defining what is already known about a site and then asking what are the gaps in this knowledge that can be filled by further investigation.

It sounds counter-intuitive for an archaeologist to say 'don't touch the archaeology'. Surely the best way to push forward the frontiers of our archaeological knowledge is to dig? In some circumstances this is indeed true, and future chapters will examine when and why archaeologists do undertake excavations. However, like a doctor who does not want to subject a patient to the trauma of surgery unless absolutely necessary, archaeologists

Below Maps record landscape features that are themselves evidence of past activities. Archaeologists look for shapes and patterns that look like the result of human activity, rather than natural forces, such as circular burial mounds, terracing or ditched enclosures.

strive to avoid causing any harm or damage to the buried archaeology if they can extract information by some other means. Instead, the aim is to use the least harmful and least costly research techniques to answer your questions efficiently, which is why the starting point for much archaeological enquiry is a desk in a library or records office, looking at maps and aerial photographs or following up clues in old photographs or archives, rather than out in the open air with a trowel.

Desktop analysis

The first phase of information gathering is referred to as 'desktop analysis' or 'desktop assessment'. You might think that this involves analysing

Above Your local library, records offices and local history archives are a good place to begin when searching for a record of the past. They are often very helpful to new users.

the debris scattered across your desk! In fact, to do so would be an archaeological exercise in its own right, treating the objects on the desk and their relation to each other as clues to your personality, lifestyle and interests. In fact, desktop analysis is the term that archaeologists use to draw a distinction between office-based research and research carried out on site, which is called 'fieldwork'.

Among the resources that are typically analysed and summarized as part of a desktop assessment are modern and historic maps, place names, records of past finds from the study area, published and unpublished excavation reports, research papers in archaeological journals, university dissertations and theses. The excavation and finds records held by planning authorities or museums (sometimes called 'Sites and Monuments Records' or 'Historic Environment Records'), aerial photographs and the maps, documents and photographs held in records offices and local history archives are analysed, too.

Making a start

Desktop analysis is often a good way for a novice to start out in archaeology because it is an area where you cannot make damaging mistakes. Libraries, records offices and local history archives strongly encourage private research and most of them are keen

to attract new users. Many run short introductory sessions explaining what resources they have and how to get the most from them.

When you embark on desktop research, it is best to start small and work outward. You might start by finding out as much as you can about your own house before you expand outward to look at the street, the neighbourhood, village or town. Most archives are organized according to geographical location, so to find your way into the records, you will need to know the grid reference for your house, or a settlement, parish or street name. At this early stage, you might wish to compile a summary of all that is known about a particular area.

Building up an analysis

Working from the known to the unknown, you can then see what information gaps there are that you might try to investigate. Here is one example: you know from comparing two maps that a house in Jackson Lane was built before 1930 (it is shown on a map of that date, so it already existed when that map was surveyed) and after 1902 (because it is not shown on a map of that date). It is part of a group of houses of similar style in the same street, which suggests that they were all built as a single development. By studying the index of the local newspaper, you might just discover an advertisement for newly built houses in

Below Past and present may be reflected in a street name: once a place where bricks were made, now famously the focus of London's Bangladeshi community.

Above Sand dredger on the River Thames near to London's Waterloo Bridge, c. 1825. Dredgermen sometimes found items in rivers that were later sold on to antiquarians.

Cabinets of curiosity

Early archaeologists were less concerned about the destructive nature of their activities than they are today. Aristocratic landowners would open up a barrow on their land to entertain their guests. To avoid possible disappointment, the barrow was sometimes excavated in advance by servants and finds put back into the soil so that the guests, journeying out to the site on horseback after lunch, could witness their 'discovery'.

Cremation urns, skulls, Roman coins or brooches excavated in this way were then placed in 'cabinets of curiosity', the forerunner to our modern museums. Road labourers, canal diggers and farm workers who made chance finds could earn a handsome bonus by selling these to local clergymen and aristocrats eager to extend their private collections. There was also a thriving trade in forging antiquities to sell at a high price to credulous antiquaries.

the street dating from 1910. The advert gives the builder's name – Thomas Jackson – which gives an explanation for the street name. You might also learn from the newspaper that he was a well-known builder of the time, so you may be able to find out what else he built in the area. Next, you could study the carved stone details that he incorporated as a signature above the front doors of his houses. They look as if they might have originally come from a much older building, so did he salvage older masonry? If so, what building or buildings did they come from and where were they? And so, as you gather more information, a fuller picture of the street's past evolves.

Below Archaeologists rely on digital maps a great deal.

Types of Maps

Accurate mapping was born out of the needs of navigation in the great age of the explorers from the 15th century. Prior to that, most surviving maps were created to facilitate the tithe system of taxation. Attempts to map the landscape in detail were mainly due to military needs arising from wars.

Above An archaeologist looks for clues on an historic county map of Wiltshire, England.

There are many reasons for the archaeologist's love affair with maps. One is that the features shown on maps – rivers, roads, settlements, woods, fields and boundaries – are exactly the same features that archaeologists study in their attempts to understand the historic environment. In other words, how people have interacted with and shaped their environment in the past, as distinct from the natural environment, which is shaped by natural forces rather than adapted by human hands.

Tithe maps and land tax

The first national British mapping agencies were established in the 18th century. Most of the maps that survive in records offices from before then are to do with land tenure and taxation. In Europe, the Church was a major landowner, and it derived much of its wealth from the tithe system, whereby landowners obeyed the Biblical instruction to pay to the Church a tithe (or one-tenth) of their income. Until the mid-19th century tithes were paid in the form of agricultural produce, such as grain, hay, timber, wine, farm animals or butter and cheese. Large tithe barns still survive in some parts of Europe for storing this produce, which then had to be sold in order to raise money for the Church. Later laws enabled the Church to convert tithes paid in kind into a financial tax, alternatively landowners could donate a piece of land to the church in perpetuity to free themselves from the annual charge.

As a result, some of the earliest maps to survive, which show details such as land boundaries, field names and the names of landowners and tenants, take the form of tithe maps. They provide a detailed picture of the countryside at the time they were surveyed, as do similar, though often less detailed, maps produced to assess landowners' liabilities to poor rates and Church rates (taxes used to pay for hospitals, almshouses, asylums and workhouses).

Enclosure, canals and railways

Another source of information is the enclosure map. It charts the change from open-field systems of farming, common throughout Europe up until the Middle Ages, to smaller hedged fields. The medieval system of common pasture that anyone could use and large fields divided into narrow strips, where each tenant grew a different crop, gave way to a system whereby the land was divided into regularly shaped fields, bounded by walls or hedges. Following an enquiry carried out by commissioners, fields were given to those individuals with demonstrable rights of land ownership within the parish. Many social injustices resulted from this system, taking land away

Left A 19th-century map showing the growth of the USA from its original 13 colonies.

Left Early mapping in the 20th century was often driven by military need. Here, an American soldier maps fire operations while sheltering in a fox hole.

National mapping agencies

The Ordnance Survey – or OS, as it is known – published its first large-scale map in 1801, and produced maps of the whole of England, Wales, Scotland and Ireland over subsequent decades. These maps are extraordinarily accurate and are at the large scale of 1:500. Published between 1855 and 1895, they are so detailed that they even show garden paths and flower-beds.

Many other countries established similar mapping agencies during the World Wars I and II, when military units mapped much of Europe and Africa. In those countries not involved in these wars, national surveys also took place, motivated by a desire to chart natural resources – such as minerals, building stone, oil and gas – and potential threats from such natural hazards as earthquakes. This was the momentum behind the mapping of the United States from 1879, of Canada from 1906, and of Australia from 1946.

from those who could not prove their title to it. However, the enclosure system did produce a legacy of maps that date from as early as the 16th century to the late 19th century.

This was also the age when trusts and companies were established to build turnpike (toll) roads, canals (England's first canal opened in 1761, the United States' in 1790) and railways (built from the 1830s in England, the United States and Australia). In each case, the production of accurate maps was an essential part of the legal process, whereby land was acquired and developed for these transport systems, and also of the engineering process to find the most efficient routes, and build tunnels, viaducts, cuttings and embankments.

Where to find historic maps online

Thanks to digitization, more and more maps are available on the Internet. For example, there are libraries such as the Perry-Castañeda Library Map Collection at the University of Texas in Austin that not only provide access to their own collections, but also provide links to tens of thousands of historic maps from all over the world. The link to the univeristy's website is www.lib.utexas.edu/maps/

Many national mapping agencies also have services on their website specifically for historians and archaeologists interested in historic maps:
• Australia, Geoscience Australia: www.ga.gov.au/
• Canada, Natural Resources Canada:
atlas.nrcan.gc.ca/site/english/index.html
• New Zealand, Land Information New Zealand:
www.linz.govt.nz
• South Africa, Chief Directorate, Surveys and Mapping:
w3sli.wcape.gov.za
• UK, Ordnance Survey: www.ordnancesurvey.co.uk
• USA, the United States Geological Survey's National Map:
nationalmap.gov/

A complete list of the world's national mapping agencies can be found at whc.unesco.org/en/mapagencies/

Above The German National Library Museum in Leipzig holds an exhaustive collection of maps covering German-speaking territories during the 20th and 21st centuries. Over 200,000 items, including giant wall maps, have been collected since 1913.

Map Regression

Comparing maps of different dates is a key archaeological technique. Known as map regression, it involves peeling away the layers of change from today's landscape and working back to the landscapes of the past to build up a picture of the ways in which settlements and landscapes have changed.

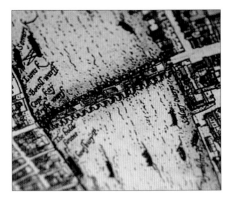

The way in which comparing maps of different periods can help to chart a period of change is perfectly illustrated by the case study of Sheffield. This industrial city in northern England, transformed from a small market town of 5,000 people, built around a Norman castle, into England's fifth largest city with a population of 1.8 million. Much of Sheffield's expansion took place during the Industrial Revolution, when the city developed an

Above Ancient property boundaries and riverside areas such as wharfs and 'bogs' are visible in this map of the Tower Bridge area of the Thames in 16th-century London.

international reputation for the quality of its iron and steel edge tools (such as files, knives and chisels) and cutlery.

Sheffield: from a rural town to a centre of industry

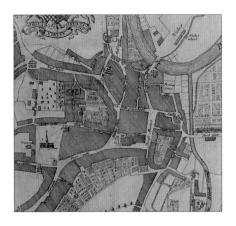

Above The map of Sheffield drawn by Gosling in 1736, mapping a hilltop town on the banks of the River Don, with just a few streets.

Above The Fairbank map of 1796 shows the original medieval core of to the east, still connected to the expanding city in the west.

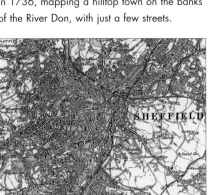

Above This OS map, not published until 1909, is based on a survey of 1887, when the city was again in a phase of rapid expansion.

Above Aerial view of modern Sheffield. The town hall (*centre*) sits just south of the site that originally contained the medieval castle.

Map regression of Sheffield

By starting with Ralph Gosling's map of Sheffield in 1736, you can see a typical rural town that is still essentially medieval in character, set on a hill above the River Don. The pattern of streets reflects the shape of the hilltop, which is oval in shape, with a long ridge spreading westward. The streets coming into the town from a number of directions follow ancient trackways across the surrounding hills, and they converge on the site of the Norman castle, church and market square.

The map of Sheffield published by Wm Fairbank and Son in 1796, and that of the Town and Environs of Sheffield published by W and J Fairbank in 1808, show how the city began to expand westward from its medieval core in the early 18th century. Growth was limited by the hilly topography, with the result that the city grew more by infilling gardens, orchards and open spaces than by outward expansion. By the mid-18th century, all of the available land within the city centre had been built upon. The first deliberately planned extensions to the city date from the 1750s: these two maps show the old western boundary of the city at Coalpit Lane and the new area of development along Division Street, with its characteristic grid-like street pattern contrasting with the more sinuous medieval streets and alleys.

In a 1903 Ordnance Survey map, you can see how the overcrowded medieval core of the city survived well into the 19th century, when comprehensive rebuilding began in 1875 – much of it was completed in time for Sheffield to be granted city status in 1893. Street widening and rebuilding gave the city centre its current character, but left key elements in the medieval street pattern intact, including narrow lanes, which vary the pattern of the city from open squares and wide boulevards to pedestrian alleyways.

Amsterdam's Canal Circle

A celebrated example of town development that can be reconstructed from maps is Amsterdam's famous *Grachtengordel*, or Canal Circle. A 16th-century aerial view of Amsterdam drawn by Cornelius Anthoniszoon (now in the Amsterdams Historische Museum) shows the medieval city, built around the dam across the River Amstel, after which the city is named. The drawing also shows the city walls and towers, separated from the strip fields beyond by a moat: the modern streets that follow the line of these defences are still called Voorburgwal and Achterburgwal, meaning 'before' and 'behind' the 'town wall'.

Amsterdam prospered on trade with Africa and the Far East to become one of Europe's biggest trading ports (along with Venice, Genoa, Lisbon, London and Antwerp). From 1609, the city council embarked on an ambitious scheme to expand the city. Three further concentric canals were dug around the medieval moat to provide space for ships to berth, warehouses and the homes of the city's merchants and bankers.

The progress of this scheme can be traced in two maps published in the 1640s, the earliest of which (*see above right*) shows that the first stretch of the canal circle has been constructed to the east of the medieval city centre, as has the new Jordaan quarter, built as an

Amsterdam: an expanding trading centre

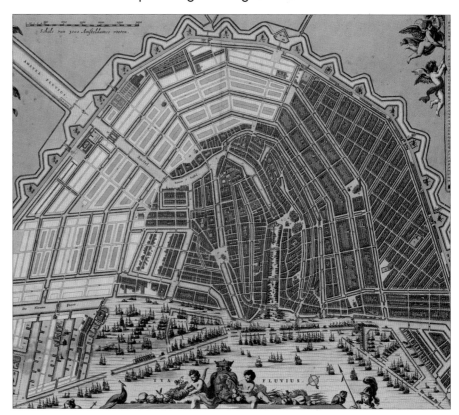

Above This map of Amsterdam shows the scheme designed by city architect Daniel Stalpaert for wrapping the Canal Circle around the original medieval heart of the city. Ships arriving at the port of Amsterdam (shown at the bottom of the map) unloaded their cargoes into barges which transported produce through the city via the canals. The coloured area of the map to the east shows how far construction had reached by the time the map was surveyed, with the western half laid out, but yet to be built.

artisans' suburb further east again, so that the prevailing westerly winds would take the smells of tanning, brewing and butchery away from the inhabited areas. A slightly later map (*see above*) shows the next stage of the canal circle dug but not yet built up, wrapping round to the north and west of the city, and terminating in an area of public parks, which are still known as Plantage ('the Plantation').

The 17th-century city has survived remarkably intact, so maps can be used to date the stylistic development of architecture in Amsterdam and create a

Above An earlier map of the city, drawn by the cartographer Joan Blaeu in the early 1640s, shows the situation before the canals were fully excavated, with long fields (called polders) to the north and west of the medieval city. The newly built Jordaan industrial quarter, planned in 1612, appears to the east.

dated archaeological-type series of gable styles, beginning with the early stepped gables, moving to bell-shaped gables and gables shaped like the shoulders and neck of a wine bottle, ending with the ornate French-style gables fashionable in the 18th century.

Maps for Dating Individual Houses

Map regression allows you to track the development of whole towns and landscapes, but equally you can compare maps to learn about the history of a specific plot or property. Whether you live in a recently built home or one that has been around for years, you're likely to find it in town plans.

Any home that has been standing for the last 100 years should be shown on a map, and possibly a copy of this will be attached to your house deeds. This is because in many parts of the world, town planning and land registers were established at the beginning of the 20th century. Sometimes there are earlier town maps to draw upon if your aim is to research an older property.

Town plans

The keeping of these records was probably thought of as intrusive and bureaucratic by some American, Australian or South African pioneers, but in retrospect they now allow researchers to trace the settlement of the US Midwest, for example, or of the earliest streets and houses in Johannesburg, in South Africa, where permission was needed from the government in Pretoria to build a house from the late 19th century. Because of this bureacracy, the maps of towns made 100 years ago are available for scrutiny and comparison with the same plots today.

In an older town, early maps and views might still exist that can take you back in time – early town plans are, for example, often found in the local history books, which were first published in reasonable quantities from the beginning of the 18th century. Such maps and engravings might appear at first sight to be crude: map makers were rarely accomplished artists and they often tried to draw a three-dimensional topographical view without the necessary skill to produce a polished perspective. Buildings are often stylized or drawn roughly, and it is tempting to dismiss many of these as inaccurate or stylized to the point where they can tell us little.

In fact, early map makers often went to great lengths to achieve accuracy, and they can be trusted to get right such details as whether the buildings they show were timber framed or built of brick or stone, whether they had gardens and back extensions, stables and orchards, and even whether they had shop fronts or inn signs.

Cirencester comparison

One town map made in 1715, by the Dutch artist and engraver Johannes Kip (1653–1722), shows part of a view of Cirencester (*see opposite page*). By comparing it with a modern photograph of the same street, it is clear from the shape of the gables and placing of the windows that the building shown in the photograph and

Above Sometimes historic maps of buildings are used as the basis of ongoing development. A project to extend the height of buildings in Wynyard Square, Sydney, incorporated information from an 1880s plan as well as a modern commercial fire-risk map.

Left Buda, the oldest part of Hungary's capital Budapest, which is divided by the River Danube, has fine examples of medieval housing.

A hidden medieval suburb

Sometimes a map shows more than what survives above ground today. Visiting the Hare Lane parking lot in Gloucester, a cathedral town by the River Severn in the west of England, you would be forgiven for thinking that the site had escaped development until recently. However, visit the local museum and you will see early maps and paintings showing that it was once a densely built-up suburb, lined by flamboyant 16th-century timber framed buildings – only two of which survive. It was flattened as part of a slum clearance programme in the 1930s and there was little subsequent development on the site, so this is an area of great interest to archaeologists looking for surviving Roman remains. Because there has been no intrusive development, with deep piles or underground parking lots, there is likely to be a rich deposit of medieval archaeology surviving below ground.

Left The Raven Inn, painted by Robert Swan in 1942 and later pulled down as part of an urban scheme, is a fine example of Hare Lane's original medieval heritage.

the one in Kip's engraving are the same. Thus, we can say with some confidence that the building must date from before 1715.

Applying this same principle to all the houses in Cirencester, you could produce a map of every building in the town shown on Kip's engraving and, therefore, existing in 1715 – in effect, making a map of the oldest buildings to survive in the town. However, more than that: having pinned down the oldest buildings, which make up about 10 per cent of all Cirencester's buildings, you can then use later maps to allocate a timespan to all the rest of the buildings, based on the date at which every building in the town makes its first appearance on a map.

As well as producing a phased series of maps that shows the town's development, map regression can also help you track the history of a particular site, looking to see what earlier buildings stood there that have since been demolished, or finding out what a building might have been used for in the past – sometimes a simple cottage might turn out to have been a public house, a place of worship, a school or even a mill.

The archaeological value of gardens

In the case of towns with a long history, map regression can help to identify areas that might have undisturbed

Above This house (*shown centre*), with its four distinctive gables, is shown on Johannes Kip's early 18th-century engraving of Cirencester, UK, at the western edge of the town.

archaeology. The Roman town of Corinium Dobunorum in England (modern-day Cirencester) had a walled area that was second only in extent to that of the Roman capital, Londinium. This large town in Roman times shrank to one-quarter of its size in the Middle Ages and did not expand again to fill the area occupied by the Roman town until the late 19th century.

Archaeologists studying the town are especially interested in houses with generous gardens that have not been touched or built upon since Roman times. In fact, that is exactly the sort of site that some of the finest mosaic pavements have been found in recent decades – on the sites of gardens, allotments and school playing fields.

Above Little changed in appearance, here is the same building today. The fact that it is on Kip's map means that the house must date from before 1715, the year the map was published.

Below Although at first glance they may seem uniform in style, Amsterdam's different types of gable can help to date the city's buildings.

Placename Evidence

Maps are covered in writing as well as symbols, and the writing — mainly consisting of placenames — is an important source of archaeological information in its own right. Placename analysis grew from the study of linguistics in the 19th century and is now an international activity.

Above Pictish placenames, as well as their standing stones, characterize central Scotland.

Specialists in toponomastics (the term for 'the study of placenames') aim to explain the origin and meaning of settlement names, and many provide dates and manuscript sources for the earliest known use of that name. Some scholars even look at the names of individual houses, farms, fields, roads, tracks and hills, woods and forests, brooks, rivers and estuaries and pubs — any topographical feature in the landscape that has a recorded name.

Prehistoric names

In some parts of Europe, placenames can be traced back to prehistory. In France, the cities of Amiens, Rheims and Soissons are examples of places that have preserved their pre-Roman

Below Roman architecture in Saintes, southern France, whose name is a corruption of the Roman name Mediolanum Santonum, meaning 'the central town of the Santones', the pre-Roman tribe that inhabited the region.

Gaulish tribal names (the homes, respectively, of the Ambiani, the Remi and the Suesiones).

In the 'Celtic fringe' of Europe — north-west Spain, western France, Cornwall, Wales, Ireland and parts of Scotland — hundreds of prehistoric names survive because these regions escaped colonization by Romans and post-Roman invaders from Central Europe. One of the most common placename elements in such names is the prefix *tre*, meaning 'hamlet', 'homestead' or 'settlement'. The second element often tells us the founder's name — for example, Tregavethan is Gavethan's homestead — or describes the local topography — Tregair is the hamlet of the *caer* ('hillfort').

In Scotland, placenames have been used to map the Kingdom of the Picts, the people who lived in northern and central Scotland in the post-Roman period. Some Pictish placenames are similar to names found in Wales — *aber*, for example, meaning 'river mouth', as in Aberdeen, or *lhan*, as in Lhanbryde, meaning 'churchyard' — but pure Pictish names include *pit* (a 'farm' or 'land-holding'), as in Pittodrie and Pittenween, *fin* ('hill'), as in Findochty, *pert* ('hedge'), as in Perth and Larbert and *carden* ('wood'), as in Kincardine.

European conquerors

In Europe and many parts of the Mediterranean, the Romans had a huge influence on placenames, either because they created cities that had not existed before (London, or the Roman Londinium, being a famous example) or because the monuments they built

were so durable that later people named the place after the Roman remains: Chester, Lancaster and Manchester, for example, from the Latin *castra*, or 'fort'; Cirencester, from 'the *castra* on the River Churn'; Eccles, from *ecclesia* ('church'), Portchester combines Latin *portus* ('harbour') and *castra*, and all the placenames beginning with 'pont' are from *pontus* ('bridge'), such as Pontefract or Pontypool.

Once Roman rule broke down in Europe, Germanic, central European and Slavic people migrated into the former empire and brought their own linguistic contribution to placenames, introducing elements such as *wald* ('wood'), *ey* ('island') and *feld* ('field'). Placenames that are distinctive to a particular group of invaders help us to identify the areas where they settled. In southern England, many places tell us that they owe their origins to the Anglo-Saxons because they include elements such as *ton* and *wic* or *wick*, which means 'settlement'. Other common Saxon placenames feature *bourne* ('stream'), *coombe* ('valley'), *worth* ('fenced enclosure'), *den* or *ling* ('hill') and *ham* ('village').

There is a clear boundary between southern names and northerly names of Viking origin that appear throughout Lincolnshire and Yorkshire up to the Scottish borders, where placenames include the elements *gate* ('road'), *beck* ('stream'), *thwaite* ('forest clearing'), *tarn* ('lake'), *garth* ('enclosure'), *fell* ('hill') and *booth* ('summer pasture').

Some well-known placenames
• Den Haag (The Hague) means 'the hedge', a reference to the fact that this used to be a royal park used for hunting, surrounded by a substantial hedge to keep the deer inside.
• Paris is named after the Parisii, the pre-Roman tribe that occupied the region where the city now lies.
• New York is named after the Duke of York, later King James II of England, but Manhattan comes from the Native American name 'Man a ha tonh', meaning the place for gathering bows.
• The Americas are either named after the Florentine explorer, Amerigo Vespucci, who first surveyed the coastline of the New World, or after the Bristol merchant Richard Amerike, who funded John Cabot's voyage of discovery to North America in 1497.

Above Spike Island, Ireland, the penal colony which lent its name to a particularly spartan housing development in the mid- to late-19th century in Sawston, Cambridgeshire, England.

Placenames with French elements do not mean that they were founded after the Norman Conquest, as they are often blended with older placename elements, as in Chester le Street, which combines French and Latin (*castra*, 'fort', and *street*, 'a paved road').

The New World
Placenames can also give us a clue to the origins of settlers and migrants in other parts of the world. Migrants have taken the names of their original homes and spread them around the world, from New England and Harlem to New Zealand and New South Wales. Although placenames can provide clues to the origin of the settlers, as in New Plymouth, this is not a consistent principle and some cities are named after a founder, patron or monarch, as in Jamestown (named after King James I of England).

In the United States, the colonization process can be traced in the European origins of placenames for the earlier settlements. The 21 states along the eastern side of the country have names derived from Latin, English, Spanish or French personal or placenames; for example, Vermont (French for 'green mountain'), Florida (Spanish for 'flowery') or Virginia (named after Elizabeth I, Queen of England).

The further west you travel, the more you will encounter placenames derived from the indigenous languages of the Native American people living in those lands, as in Missouri, from *mihsoori*, 'dugout canoe', Utah, meaning 'high land' or Mississippi, derived from the native American Ojibwe word *misi-ziibi* meaning 'great river'.

In some parts of the world, our more enlightened age has decided to revert to indigenous names, as in Mount Cook in New Zealand, named in honour of Captain James Cook, who first circumnavigated New Zealand in 1770, but now called Aoraki, meaning 'cloud piercer', in the Kai Tahu dialect of the Maori language.

Recent names
Names do not have to be old to convey information: street names and house names can help with dating, from the numerous places all over the former British Empire that commemorate Queen Victoria, to those that remind us of battles and military leaders, or have origins in folklore. For example, 'The Spike' in the Cambridgeshire village of Sawston is named after Spike Island, an Irish open prison used between 1847 and 1883; Sawston's 'Spike' can be dated to this period. The name tells us what the tanning factory workers of Sawston, who named the district, thought of their new homes.

Below Migrants from the Old World to the New found many familiar placenames on arrival in their new environments.

Patterns in the Landscape

As well as being a useful tool for charting and dating the growth in settlements, maps also have another important function to archaeologists. These representations of the landscape can help to identify patterns and shapes that might be of archaeological significance once interpreted.

The landscape is an amalgam of natural and human actions. Contours and gradients, watercourses and vegetation are mainly the result of natural processes, but much else in the landscape is the result of human activity, whether it be in the form of planted woodland, cultivated fields, field boundaries, ditches and artificial watercourses, or quarries, harbours, roads and buildings. An archaeologist, reading a map, is interested in the patterns that indicate human interaction with the landscape. Though many landscape alterations will be modern, there are a surprising number that are far older.

Below Roman roads, like the Appian Way in Puglia, southern Italy, are easy to distinguish on maps because of their straightness.

Patterns with meaning

Over time, archaeologists (especially those who specialize in landscape history) have become skilled at interpreting maps to find the older patterns that tell a story of settlement growth and land use. Their work is based on the assumption that certain basic principles underlie the way that people have used the landscape in the past, and that many of these uses leave distinctive patterns.

Property boundaries and hedge lines generally leave behind noticeable patterns. Historic railways and canals, ancient droveways and Roman roads are also easy to spot on a map, even where they have been closed or abandoned for years, because their linear character survives and is

Above Ancient walled boundaries and gently sloping banks in Dartmoor, southern England.

apparent in the property boundaries or hedge alignments that remain.

Boundaries as a whole are a rich field of study, and some archaeologists, by combining fieldwork and map study, have been able to show that some types of field patterns survive from the prehistoric period in Europe, especially in upland areas that were once cultivated, but are now used for grazing. These ancient land divisions were first recognized on Dartmoor, the extensive area of granite upland at the centre of the English county of Devon. In Dartmoor the low walls and banks, known locally as 'reaves', run in parallel lines down valley slopes, dividing the land into narrow strips. They have been excavated and dated to the Bronze Age. Similar land divisions dating from approximately the same period are now being discovered in other upland areas of Europe – in the Causse Méjan region of south-central France, for example.

Other patterns might be based on topographical principles. One example would be that springs occur at specific places where the underlying geology changes: find those springs and you will probably also find archaeological sites because springs have often been regarded as sacred places in the past. Roman farms and villas are also located close to a spring, and are often built halfway up a gentle south-facing slope, aligned east to west.

Some patterns are characteristic of a particular time or culture. All over

Right The sheer size of Long Bredy in Dorset, southern England, makes it a striking landmark – it is a Neolithic barrow some 197m (645ft) long and 1.8m (6ft) high. However, its immediate surroundings reveal other interesting, less obvious archaeology from different periods, such as circular Bronze Age round barrows, ditches and cross-dykes that marked out ancient pasture.

Europe and the Mediterranean, archaeologists have worked out the extent of Roman colonization simply by looking at maps for the tell-tale signs of straight roads and towns with a strict rectilinear street plan aligned on the cardinal points of the compass. Even the extent of Roman farming can be plotted by looking for rectilinear fields aligned with the course of Roman roads characteristic of the Roman system of land division known as 'centuriation'. This pattern can still be seen clearly, for example, in the flatlands of the Po River delta in northern Italy, east of Ferrara and north of Ravenna.

Mysterious patterns

Other patterns are more subtle and there is not always an explanation. Archaeologists are still trying to uncover the principles that might underlie the positioning of prehistoric burial mounds in the landscape. An archaeologist might question what made people choose this spot rather than that? Once it was thought that burial mounds were placed on hilltops and ridges to be visible from afar. Studying the map suggests that this might be true – where you find clusters of mounds along the escarpment of the Cotswolds in England, for example. However, many mounds have been found in low-lying areas, and environmental evidence from ancient pollens in the soil of the burial mound tells us that some were built in woodland clearings, where they wouldn't be seen by anyone who didn't know where to look.

The archaeologist, therefore, has to be careful when studying maps to avoid producing patterns where there are none. These sites might have been

Above The Po River delta in Itay has a flat landscape and a system of lagoons (or polders) that has seen a history of intensive farming.

chosen by divination or there might have been no rational pattern at all. Or is there some other pattern? Some archaeologists have observed that some classes of mound have been found precisely 1.6km (1 mile) in a south-easterly direction from the nearest contemporary settlement.

Another challenge to the map interpreter is the fact that the landscape is dynamic and might have looked different in the past. Rivers in particular have a habit of changing their course, especially if there are wide plains that offer a choice of routes, or where glaciation has

The elephant-shaped hill

Not all patterns have an archaeological explanation. The British Library has a map of Africa's Gold Coast surveyed in 1923 with a hill that looks like an elephant. In fact, that is exactly what it is. Toiling under the tropical sun all day, the soldiers responsible for surveying this inaccessible region must have decided that they had done enough. Rather than survey the blank area on the map, they filled it in by drawing round a picture in a magazine, creating contours in the form of an elephant. Perhaps because so few people visit this part of Africa, the elephant-shaped hill remained undetected for many years.

significantly changed the shape of the landscape. Some archaeologists – called palaeo-environmentalists – specialize in creating maps of the ancient landscape. They look for the typical contours that mark sites of earlier curves of the rivers, or of ancient lakes, such as Lake Mungo and the Willandra lakes in Australia, where evidence of early human settlement might be found.

Aerial Views of Buried Features

Early aerial photography was designed to give earthbound archaeologists a better view of standing monuments, but it also reveals buried features. Archaeologists routinely use photographs taken from the air to look for soil marks, shadows and crop marks reflecting what lies beneath the soil.

Above This crater-like landscape in eastern England is evidence of Neolithic flint mining.

Experimenting with balloons, scaffolds and kites, and then using aeroplanes as a vantage point, archaeologists have been taking photographs from the air for more than a century, motivated initially by the desire to see large monuments in their entirety and within their wider setting. However, a very different revolution was born once archaeologists realized that not only could they see standing monuments, but they could also detect buried features and sites barely recognizable from the ground.

How buried features shape the land

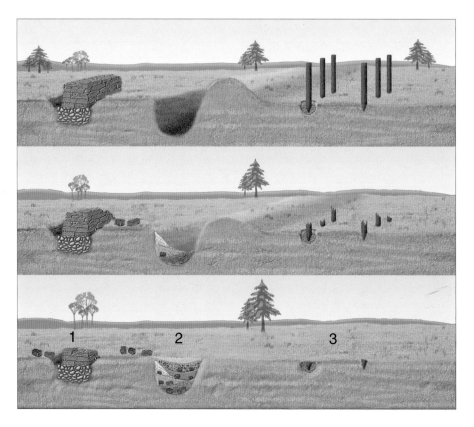

Above This series of illustrations demonstrates how the gradual decay of features impacts on the landscape. **1** Buried walls lead to stunted crops because the roots lack moisture and cannot penetrate the deeper soil. **2** Ditches have the opposite effect, providing deep moist soil and taller crops. **3** Post holes and post pits produce taller crops, and a pattern of shadows all in a row.

Revealing new archaeological sites

Until the 1920s, the only way to find archaeological sites was by chance – builders stumbling across a Roman mosaic or farmer's ploughing up flint tools – or through the ditches, banks, walls and mounds, monuments and materials that happened to survive above ground. With the arrival of aerial photography, the archaeologist has been given the ability to see beneath the soil and detect buried features from the air, the equivalent of giving an archaeologist X-ray vision. One immediate consequence was a huge rise in the number of known archaeological sites. Slowly, maps that had been virtually empty of archaeological sites, began to fill. For the first time ever in human history, people began to realize just how intensively the landscape had been used in the past, how many sites there were, and how large past populations might have been.

Weather and soil patterns

There are many different reasons why buried features can, under certain conditions, be seen from the air. Soil marks are the simplest to see, and they depend on the contrast in colour, between the natural geology and buried features, that is revealed when a site is ploughed. Such contrasts are especially noticeable in chalky soils, where the dark rings of ditches and burial mounds, pits, hut circles or enclosure ditches contrast vividly with the white colour of the surrounding topsoil.

Parch marks

Apart from soil colour differences, most of the other features visible on aerial photographs have to do with weather and soil depth and their effects on natural or cultivated vegetation. Parch marks, for example, often tell us where stone walls, floors, paths or burial chambers can be found, because the grass growing above is denuded of moisture and turns yellow when the spring rains cease, temperatures rise and moisture in the soil evaporates under the dehydrating effects of the sun. Such colour differences might only last a few days, before all the grass begins to parch and turn yellow, but if you happen to catch the fleeting moment of maximum contrast, the amount of detail revealed can be astonishing. Lost and buried towns, villages, churches, villas, farmsteads, garden terraces and paths, cemeteries, forts and monastic complexes have all been discovered in this way.

Crop marks

Another way to find archaeological remains is through crop marks. Minor colour differences can result from differential crop germination and access to water. Seed planted over pits and

Below Patterns made by parch marks and ditches reveal the remains of an entire ancient settlement – in this case, the deserted medieval village of Middle Ditchford in the Cotswolds area of western England. The long shadows indicate the low angle of the sun at the time of photography.

Above O.G.S. Crawford combined extensive flying experience and archaeology to become the pioneer of aerial archaeology.

Pioneer of aerial photography

O.G.S. (Osbert Guy Stanhope) Crawford (1886–1957) served as an observer with the Royal Flying Corps in Europe in World War I. He was shot down in 1918, but survived and was appointed the first Archaeology Officer of the Ordnance Survey in 1920, responsible for compiling the archaeological information that appears on British Ordnance Survey maps.

Crawford combined his love of photography with his flying experience to create a new discipline. He wrote *Air Survey and Archaeology* (1924) and *Air Photography for Archaeologists* (1929), which brought his work to the attention of archaeologists in other parts of the world. Previously unsuspected discoveries began to be made worldwide – from the astonishing Nazca Lines of Peru, rediscovered in 1939 by the US archaeologists Dr Paul Kosok and Maria Reiche, to the subtle remains of prehistoric footpaths and roads in Central America and the 6,000 surviving Maori earthwork fortifications (called pā in Maori) that have now been mapped from the air in New Zealand.

ditches will often germinate slightly earlier than neighbouring plants, resulting in subtle colour differences at certain points in the growing season, as the plants mature at different rates. Crops that germinate earlier will be darker in the three weeks or so before they begin to ripen and vice versa: seed sown on the stony ground of a burial mound, cairn, bank or buried wall will be lighter and later to mature.

In addition, deep features such as pits and ditches act as a sump, attracting and retaining moisture, while shallower soil dries out under the sun. This can further exaggerate colour differences in the crop, or even result in taller crops that throw a slight shadow if photographed when the sun is low in the sky, revealing the presence, location and shape of buried archaeology (*see opposite page*).

The effects of shadow

Parch marks produce 'negative' marks that appear as lighter lines on photographs, whereas crop marks are visible as 'positive', or darker, lines. Parch marks and crop marks are usually most numerous from late spring to early autumn, but winter brings an entirely new set of conditions because lush vegetation that might disguise the presence of mounds and hollows dies down, and the low angle of the sun produces shadow marks revealing slight differences in contour. In full sunlight, for example, a buried farmstead might simply look like a rectangular platform; low winter sun can reveal individual buildings grouped around a courtyard.

Snow and flooding

Flooding, snow and frost can produce similar effects to shadows. Water lying in the shallow features of a field can reveal buried pits, ditches, ploughing lines, boundaries, ponds and water scoops; while frost and snow that collects, drifts and melts at different rates can emphasize subtle differences in height between features. Garden archaeology, for example, often involves studying winter photographs to detect ponds and mounds, alleys and terraces, paths and beds, wild and cultivated ground.

Mapping the Results

To maximize the benefits of aerial photography, archaeologists need to be able to transcribe the features they can see on to a map. To do this means using various pieces of equipment and various techniques that minimize the distortions of contour, angle and perspective.

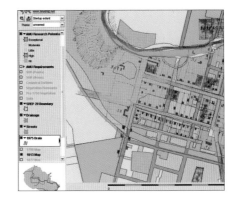

Purely for reconnaissance purposes – just recording what is visible on the ground – 'oblique' photographs will do, and many air photographic collections have huge collections of such pictures, which can be taken simply by pointing a hand-held camera through the window of a light aircraft. They are called 'oblique' because they are taken at an oblique, or slanting, angle to the landscape.

However, if the features are to be mapped, it is necessary to take 'vertical' photographs, which requires a plate camera to be mounted on or within the plane. Gyroscopes and levelling instruments ensure that the camera stays level, even if the aeroplane itself tilts, and the camera is set to photograph a block of landscape directly below the plane. Sometimes pairs of cameras are mounted side by side to take stereoscopic pictures that almost overlap, which produces a three-dimensional image when looked at through a special viewfinder.

Photogrammetry

Even vertical photography has to be rectified before the features that are visible on the print can be super-imposed on to a base map, because the ground itself is very rarely completely flat. When measuring how long a wall or ditch might be, for example, compensation has to be made for the effect of landscape relief as the wall or ditch runs uphill or down a valley. Specialist plotting machines and computer programmes have been developed that take on much of the repetitive arithmetic involved in transcription work (technically known as 'photogrammetry' – the conversion of vertical photographs into accurate scaled plans).

Above In 2000, an initiative to incorporate the archaeological heritage of Australia's second mainland settlement, Parramatta, into plans for the city's development used GIS to align and display current streets and boundaries, archaeological features and a sequence of historic maps and aerial photographs. The resulting plan was then incorporated into a heritage inventory database.

Film types

Black-and-white film is much used in aerial photography because it is inexpensive and easy to process, as well as because it gives good clear results that can be manipulated easily to heighten contrasts.

Infrared film is also used because it heightens the contrast in colours – such as the colours in crop marks – so that very slight variations can be seen more clearly than they would appear in 'true' colour or in black and white photography. However, when inter-preting infrared prints, you have to get used to the counter-intuitive fact that green represents plough soil and red represents crops.

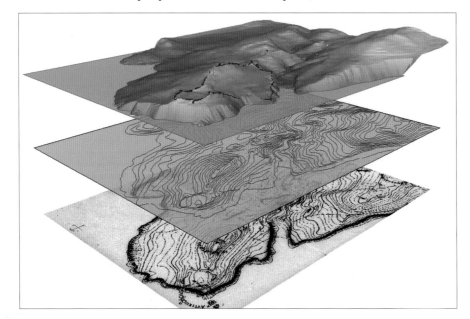

Left Topographic information and GIS are used to construct a three-dimensional view of a Hellenistic fort on the island of Antekythera, Greece. The topographic data (including contours and other details of the landscape), shown at the bottom level, is 'traced' and integrated with a plan of the fort created by walking around the ruins with a global positioning system. This tracing appears as the middle level. Using GIS, the tracing is projected onto three dimensions to give an idea of what the walls and towers, in red, would have looked like (top level).

Geographical Information Systems

One of the biggest innovations in mapping of recent years has to be the use of computerized Geographical Information Systems (GIS), a computer system for storing and displaying mapped data. Although GIS sounds complex, it is really a simple idea. Instead of storing information on a computer by placename or monument type, it is labelled with map coordinates – degrees of longitude and latitude – so that it can be stored spatially. This allows the information to be superimposed upon a base map, which makes it is easier for you to find what you are interested in, simply by locating the specific area you want on the computer map and selecting from a menu of information.

The work of transcribing archaeological data from photographs on to maps and interpreting the features on the basis of their shape and size and relationship to each other is a highly skilled activity that requires training and expensive equipment. However, once the different features are coded, they are stored as different layers of information, and the data from hundreds of photographs can be brought together in one GIS system. At that point anyone can use the system to produce richly detailed pictures of the landscape and its archaeological features at different periods in time.

Revealing continuity

This data in a GIS system can be superimposed over the top of the modern landscape, often with fascinating results. Sometimes the landscape has been so radically transformed by later activity that there is no discernible link between the present and the past, but equally it is often the case that features visible above ground – hedges, walls, ditches, and other boundary markers, for example – line up with buried features, revealing, for example, that a particular wall marking a parish boundary dates back hundreds, if not thousands, of years.

Mapping Angkor Wat's historic canal system

The restoration of Angkor Wat, Cambodia, including original canals and roadways, formed the basis of a UNESCO-funded survey during the mid-1990s. More recently, the Archaeological Computing Laboratory at the University of Sydney imported this information, along with aerial photography and remote sensed images (such as satellite images and airborne radar imagery), into a GIS system to identify archaeological features at the site.

Above An aerial photograph of Angkor reveals a landscape of modern fields and roads, mounds and *trapeang* (ponds).

Above At ground level, measurements of individual buildings are taken to check the accuracy of earlier drawings.

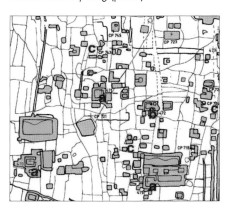

Above Archaeological features are traced from remote sensed data. The blue areas are the *trapeang* and moats; the brown areas are mounds; black lines show field boundaries.

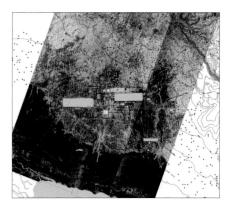

Above A digitized map combining information on contours, radar imagery and archaeological features. The pale blue rectangles are Angkorean period reservoirs.

The future lies with Lidar

The use of digital aerial photography is in its infancy, but promises astonishing results, especially when associated with light detection and ranging (Lidar) technology. Lidar uses laser pulses bouncing off the surface of the earth to detect solid bodies, just as radar uses radio waves. Mounted on an aeroplane, Lidar scanners measure the time it takes for the signal to bounce back from the earth, scanning the ground surface to an accuracy of 154mm (6in).

Lidar can see through clouds and thick woodland or vegetation and can be used year round, day and night. Its ability to see through jungle foliage has made a huge difference to archaeology in South America, where normal aerial photography is impossible. Lidar, however, is not invincible: it is not as effective in areas with peaty soils and gravels that do not reflect laser pulses well.

The Value of Inventories

Although they are little more than lists of known sites and monuments, inventories provide varying levels of descriptive and analytical detail. They are another important resource for anyone trying to find out as much as possible about the archaeology of a particular area.

Archaeologists have been making lists since the earliest days of the discipline. When the venerable Society of Antiquaries was founded in London in 1707, one of its first tasks was to compile 'a comprehensive survey of the nation's antiquities'. This goal, of creating a definitive list, or inventory, of all known archaeological sites has proved to be elusive: not only are sites discovered (and destroyed) faster than people can record them, the definition of 'archaeology' continues to widen.

In the last 50 years, we have seen the rise of industrial and marine archaeology, and prisons, cold-war military sites, shops and suburban houses are a few examples of what are now classed as heritage sites.

Legal duty

Inventories are so fundamental to archaeology that new laws are currently being drafted in Britain, making it a legal duty for all planning authorities to maintain accurate and

Above Inventories of Canada's heritage include records of human activity as well as monuments, like this photograph of a Native American gathering at Red River, Hudson Bay.

up-to-date inventories. Many already do so, and they are known as Sites and Monuments Records (SMRs) or by the more modern name of Historic Environment Records (HERs).

These records play a critical role in ensuring that nobody destroys an archaeological site out of ignorance. When somebody applies for planning permission to build on a site, the register is checked to see if anything archaeological has ever been found there in the past. As well as having this practical application within the planning system, SMRs or HERs are also of great value to anyone researching any part of the historic landscape. Anyone can ask to see them, although usually this involves making an appointment, and some local authorities are keen to see greater use made of their inventories in academic and voluntary research.

SMRs and HERs seek to record all the known sites in a defined geographical area, so your first task as a researcher interested in a particular site is to find out where the relevant list is held – a good starting point is to look at the website of your local planning authority, under 'Planning' or 'Conservation Services'.

Other national inventories

Britain is exceptional in having such comprehensive local and regional coverage, though Australia, Canada and

Above and right Some inventories are set up by organizations keen to recover traditional knowledge, for example on ancient hunting techniques or water conservation. The structures shown here formed part of Italian researcher Pietro Laureano's 'Water Atlas' project.

New Zealand, along with some American states, also have similar regional record systems, and most countries in the world have inventories at national level of the sites and monuments that are of sufficient importance to be 'listed' or 'designated'.

Studying inventories

The site you are interested in might also feature a number of other inventories that have been compiled by archaeologists over the last century or more as part of research into a particular monument type. For example, you might find inventories that are devoted to standing stones, rock art, burial mounds, hillforts, Roman villas, early Christian churches, medieval deer parks, battlefields, windmills, munitions factories or hospitals and asylums.

If you are lucky, the task of consulting all these inventories might be made easier for you by cross references from one source to another. In a good modern inventory, individual entries will not only describe what is known about the site, it will also include a list of references to published and unpublished records – for example, excavation reports or other inventories.

The quality of inventories will vary greatly, and you might find looking through inventories for information about a site something of a lucky dip.

Left Maori wood carvings, such as this one at Paihia, are among the artefacts listed as Protected in New Zealand's national inventory.

Where to find inventories

To find out what archaeological databases and inventories exist and where they can be consulted, it is best to start with the website of the relevant government agency: it might be a national state heritage service, or it might be the heritage and planning department of the state, regional, county or district government. The websites of state heritage services will often point you toward other local and regional sources of information.

- Australia: The Department of the Environment and Heritage (DEH) www.deh.gov.au/
- Canada: The Canadian Heritage Information Network: www.chin.gc.ca/English/index.html
- England, English Heritage: www.english-heritage.org.uk/ (the National Monuments Resource Centre run by English Heritage in Swindon is a good starting point as it has its own inventories resulting from 100 years of fieldwork and it works in partnership with a number of other archive and record-holding bodies and so has indexes to the records that they hold)
- England, the Archaeology Data Service: ads.ahds.ac.uk/ (the ADS has a large and growing range of databases, including HEIRNET, which has details of National Monuments Records, Sites and Monuments Records, national thematic inventories, specialist resources and other information sources held by organisations from across the UK)
- New Zealand, The Ministry for Culture and Heritage: www.mch.govt.nz/; New Zealand Archaelogical Association: www.nzarchaeology.org/
- Northern Ireland, The Environment and Heritage Service: www.ehsni.gov.uk/
- Republic of Ireland, The Department of the Environment, Heritage and Local Government: www.heritagedata.ie/en/
- Scotland, The Royal Commission on the Ancient and Historical Monuments of Scotland: www.rcahms.gov.uk/
- South Africa, South African Heritage Resources Agency: www.sahra.org.za/intro.htm
- Wales, The Royal Commission on the Ancient and Historical Monuments of Wales: www.rcahmw.org.uk/

Just as it is impossible to compile a definitive inventory, so it is impossible to consult every inventory that exists on the off-chance that it might throw light on your site.

A good example of an inventory is the site recording scheme run by the New Zealand Archaeological Association (see box above). It will enable anyone – amateur, academic or professional – to consult or contribute to a growing database of sites, ranging from Maori settlements and houses to shipwrecks and whaling industry remains. Their inventory includes, for example, comprehensive coverage of MÇori pÇ (pronounced pah), which are vital defended hilltop settlements surrounded by earthen ramparts.

Remember, too, that compiling inventories is an important activity for archaeologists in its own right and one where amateurs can make a significant contribution. There are active groups all over the world that record everything from church monuments and tombstone inscriptions to war memorials or defensive structures surviving from World Wars I and II. In fact, for every class of world heritage, from historic millstones to early examples of chapels and houses built from corrugated iron, there is more than likely to be a club or society devoted to making an inventory of surviving examples.

Miscellaneous Records

As well as consulting inventories to find out what is already known about a site, a conscientious archaeologist will comb through a huge and bewildering array of archives, books, journals and digital databases, and check the holdings of museums, local studies libraries and records offices.

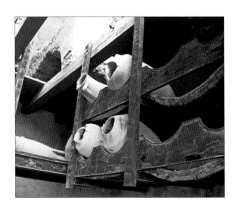

People who use and manage heritage information systems dream of the day when comprehensive and fully indexed records are available on-line, so that all you have to do is enter a placename or grid coordinate into a search engine to retrieve everything that is known about a site. However, we are a long way yet from the day when the world's archaeological data can be consulted in one big seamless on-line database. Until that happens, learning about a

Above Museums with sizeable archaeological collections may be able to give information on many artefacts not actually on display.

particular site more often means making an appointment to go and visit a museum, records office or a local library and trawling through the records that they maintain.

Museum archives

If the house, street, settlement or landscape you are studying is the site of a major archaeological monument, it is likely that you will be following in the trail of several previous archaeologists who will probably have left plenty of information to follow up. Looking for

Above and left Prior to excavating part of the grounds at Berkeley Castle, western England, archaeologists at the University of Bristol used existing historical records to research the original landscape, including a Tudor map (Moyle's 1544 survey of Berkeley, *left*) and a 1712 town plan (by Jan Kip, *above*).

Below This 17th-century painting of Berkeley Castle by Hendrick Dankerts provided further clues to the castle's geography and the possible location of a medieval road.

Above A recently published article or book will list the sources or archives the author has consulted in the footnotes and bibliography.

Footnotes and bibliographies

Archaeology is a scientific discipline, and like all sciences, it proceeds on the basis of a separation between data and interpretation. In the case of archaeology, the data often consists of material that has already been published somewhere else. Rather than repeat what is already available, footnotes and bibliographies are used to show where that data can be found.

This academic practice is of enormous benefit to anyone trying to finding a way through the maze of material that might exist for the area being studied. The footnotes and bibliography will give leads worth following up, and each one will have its own footnotes and bibliography, pointing you in all sorts of directions for further research.

Above Public libraries and records offices may have a computerized database of maps, deeds, wills and other valuable sources.

information is more of a challenge if you are the first to study an area, or if the finds are not spectacular enough to feature in published literature or museum displays – bones and flints, for example, rather than fine brooches or pottery. Most museums have room after room of these less glamorous finds, and the amount of material stored in basements and back rooms is often several times greater than the amount on display.

Some museums are now pursuing the enlightened path of opening up their stores and encouraging their use. Anyone researching the archaeology of Greater London, for example, can visit the London Archaeological Archive Resource Centre (LAARC; www.museumoflondon.org.uk/laarc/new/default.asp) and look at material and records from over 5,000 projects in the city, dating back to the beginning of the 20th century.

LAARC is a pioneer in providing free public access to a rich body of material; more commonly, museums are not geared to the needs of researchers and the quality and completeness of their archives can vary. In some cases, records may consist of little more than a shoebox full of card indexes with handwritten details of accidental finds, such as a Roman coin found by someone digging their vegetable patch and brought to the museum for identification. At the other end of the scale, records can consist of detailed computerized records linked to finds, photographs, maps, plans, excavation reports, analyses and references to other books and sources for further information about the site.

Records and local archives

Though archaeology, in its emphasis on the study of material remains, is a separate discipline from local history, based on documentary research, it would be foolish to ignore what historical records might be able to tell you about a site or landscape. There are no hard and fast boundaries between archaeological and historical methodology at the desktop assessment phase of the research process – the differences come to the fore once archaeologists move into the field. So a desktop assessment will include a search through records that are held in a records office or a local history library.

These might include copies of old newspapers, historic photographs, census returns, deeds and wills, parish registers, charters and grants of land, and possibly diaries and antiquarian field notes, paintings and engravings that show streets, buildings, towns or monuments as they looked in the past, or the papers of large estates or ecclesiastical authorities.

None of this should be neglected as a possible source of information, even if it takes time to work systematically through the indexes looking for relevant material. Such a search is more likely to prove rewarding if you are studying the comparatively recent past, especially if you want to add a human dimension to your knowledge. Archaeologists in London, for example, excavating houses that were destroyed by wartime bombing, were able to date the construction of buildings from newspaper reports, put names to the people who lived in the houses, find out what their occupations were, excavate the pipes that previous inhabitants had smoked, the toys that their children played with and even reconstruct what they might have had for tea from the jars and bottles found in their refuse tips.

What are you looking for and why?

How far you go toward building up a complete picture depends on your field of research – some researchers become obsessive collectors of data, while others look at only recent research on the grounds that current archaeological methods yield more reliable data than past antiquarian pursuits. The aim in either case is to become familiar with the grain and character of the area you are studying. It takes time to do this – sometimes many months or years – but developing an archaeological feel for the landscape is satisfying and rewarding, as your mental picture begins to build up detail and nuance.

Case Study: a Cotswold Upland Farm, England

Above Geophysical equipment is used to find the precise location of buried ditches and pits.

In 2007, the School of Conservation Sciences at Bournemouth University, England, organized a line excavation at a farm in Wiggold, Gloucestershire. The dig was preceded by a detailed desktop assessment designed to reveal as much as possible about the farm's archaeological history.

The location of the excavation site at Wiggold was an important factor. Nearby Cirencester, south-west of the site, was a major Roman town linked to other Roman administration centres by a network of roads, some of which are still in use.

Placenames and documents

Akeman Street, the main Roman road from Cirencester to London, forms the farm's southern boundary, and the Fosse Way, linking Exeter to Lincoln via Bath, Cirencester and Leicester, runs north to south through the middle of the farm holding. It is possible that both roads have changed their course over time, so the farm might well have original Roman roads preserved beneath its fields, as well as possible roadside buildings.

White Way is another road of Roman, or possibly prehistoric, date that forms the western boundary of the farm. 'White Way' is a medieval name that refers to the salt that was carried

Below Archives held at the National Monuments Record Centre, Swindon, produced this aerial photograph of a mysterious circular feature, which might be an Iron Age (pre-Roman) enclosure, or the remains of a ditch and bank built to keep deer out of woodland in the Middle Ages.

along this road after being extracted from the brine wells beneath the town of Droitwich, at the northern end of this road. Welsh Way, forming the northern boundary of the farm, is named after the Welsh drovers who brought their sheep and cattle along this road heading east toward the markets of London, having crossed the River Severn at Gloucester.

Wiggold itself is a Saxon name, which means the *wold* ('wood') of someone named Wiga – perhaps the same Wiga who is recorded in the Domesday book as the owner of land in Pauntley, in Gloucestershire, and at Kilcot, on the River Thames further east in Oxfordshire. The Domesday book also records that William Fitz Osbern, Earl of Hereford, who owned Cirencester manor from 1066 to 1070, detached two hides (206ha (514 acres)) of land and bestowed them on a tenant to create the Manor of Wigwold, but the Saxon name suggests that the farm at Wiggold has origins that go back to before the Norman Conquest.

Aerial photographs

The National Monuments Record Centre houses aerial photographs that were taken over a period of 50 years. These reveal that the farm has many buried archaeological features, including the lines of medieval field boundaries, hedges and ditches that were removed in the 1950s to make larger fields, and the remains of medieval ridge and furrow cultivation, as well as many ditches and pits whose shapes suggest prehistoric enclosures.

Inventories and archives

No less than 95 known sites have been recorded in the immediate vicinity of the farm. These include burial mounds dating from the Bronze and Iron Ages and prehistoric pits, through to more recent quarries and lime kilns.

A visit to the local museum revealed that large numbers of prehistoric flints have been found at seven different parts of the farm. Additionally, Roman pottery and building material has been reported from an area of the farm that lies along the route of the old Midland and South Western Junction Railway, which ceased to operate in the 1960s and has since been turned into a farm track.

Conclusion

In the case of the Cotswold's upland farm project, desktop analysis has demonstrated that there can be a huge amount of archaeological information to be found in maps and photographs, or buried away in archives and inventories. From the analysis, it is now known that this farm has a rich

Above Field walking prior to excavation was used to identify areas in which flint tools had been made and used.

multi-period archaeological landscape, with many potentially important sites located within it.

Desktop analysis can result in a cascade of data or a complete blank. If you do draw a blank, you might worry that the area you have chosen to study lacks archaeology – in reality, it can mean that nobody has yet been out to look. Absence of data doesn't always mean absence of archaeology, so you need to move on to the next stage and undertake investigations in the field.

However, too much data might lead you to ask whether there is anything left to be discovered. The answer is yes, because most of what you find will be raw material that has yet to be digested and analysed. This data doesn't become information until someone brings it all together in one place and adds it all up into a coherent picture.

Gathering together the disparate strands of what is already known is the first step toward writing a history of the place that you live in, and all archaeological research is based on this pattern of enquiry – working from the known to the unknown. Desktop analysis – pinning down what we already know – is essential for framing the next stage in the archaeological process, when we move from the desk and the computer into the field.

Left This shallow ford across the River Severn, still in use, was once used as an important trade link by drovers taking livestock to market from their farms in Wales.

LOOKING FOR EVIDENCE IN THE FIELD

In the previous chapter, we have seen that the purpose of desktop analysis is to gather as complete a picture as possible about the site or area being studied. The next stage is to leave the desk and look at the evidence on the ground. This chapter looks at the techniques involved for getting to know your site in more detail before deciding whether or not to excavate. Although several types of high-tech equipment are used to access the landscape, the archaeologist also relies heavily on observation to help with the analysis of the site, and by simply walking across the land, there is plenty to be discovered. These first two stages – desktop analysis and looking for evidence in the field – often go hand in hand. It's often only after giving proper consideration to the evidence gathered from both stages, that a decision to dig, or not to dig, is finally made.

Opposite Archaeology students learn how to operate a global positioning system (GPS).

Above Many archaeologists now use hand-held GPS in conjunction with maps to locate earthworks as part of a field survey.

Above Heritage conservationists conducting a survey of surviving archaeology in Hampshire, UK, record their observations.

Above Walking a site where the earth has been recently tilled may turn up anything from ancient pottery shards to Roman mosaics.

From the Desk to the Field

Studying landscapes without visiting the area you are studying is like trying to write a travel guide to Vienna without visiting the city. You need to get a feel for the city's unique atmosphere, and the same is true of archaeological sites – knowing them on paper is no substitute for walking the site.

Above Archaeologists may use GPS to determine a precise area to be fieldwalked.

In reality desktop analysis and field survey go together – the two techniques are not used separately – rather, they complement each other. Archaeologists involved in archival research will constantly visit the site they are studying to compare what they have discovered from maps and photographs with what they can see on the ground, and vice versa. Looking at the landscape in the field will often suggest new questions or lines of enquiry that need to be researched using maps and databases.

High-tech surveying
Some of these techniques used to survey the field are based on remote sensing technology – using instruments such as metal detectors, global positioning systems (GPS), resistivity meters and magnetometers. This equipment was

Stone for Stonehenge
In 2004 archaeologists Geoff Wainwright and Tim Darvill set out to study the hilltop of Carn Meini in South Wales, from where the bluestones of the inner circle at Stonehenge were quarried around 2600BC. Their desktop analysis of the site produced a blank archaeological map. However, after three seasons of fieldwork they discovered hundreds of examples of prehistoric activity. Their archaeological map of the area is now crowded with cairns, causewayed enclosures, chambered long barrows, stone circles, dolmens, single standing stones and rock art, along with large areas of prehistoric quarry debris, littered with hammer stones and flake tools. The lesson is that you should never assume that because an area is well known that it has been well studied – and that simply looking at the landscape with an enquiring mind can produce rich rewards.

Right The hilltop of Carn Meini is in the Presili Hills of Pembrokeshire, South Wales.

Above Among the more visible features are prehistoric standing stones, such as the Kermario stones near Carnac, northern France, which date from the third millennium BC.

once so expensive and technical that it was used by only a handful of specialists working in university departments of archaeological science, but it is now becoming standard equipment used by all archaeologists. With the fall in price has come an equally important change – ease of use.

Walking the fields

As well as high-tech survey techniques, archaeologists also use some very simple tried-and-tested field survey methods that require very little by way of equipment and are the backbone of much amateur field archaeology. Walking over fields systematically after ploughing to look for scatters of pottery, flint, tile or bone is another commonly deployed technique for discovering sites, as is metal detecting, which has a valuable role to play in archaeology if used with respect for the archaeology rather than as a treasure-hunting device (*see* Geophysical Surveys).

Rock art

In the parts of the world where nomadic people build shelters from organic materials that leave little archaeological trace, much of our knowledge about past societies has come from 'above ground' archaeology. One important area of study is rock art, whether painted or carved. It is one of the oldest forms of human expression and one of the most widespread – from Northumberland, England, to North Africa, from South Africa to Australia, and from Chile to Ottowa. There are enthusiastic groups dedicated to finding, recording and conserving the astonishing range of what are technically called 'petroglyphs' if they

Above Detail of a bison head from a Paleolithic cave mural painting in Lascaux II grotto, France.

are incised, 'pictographs' if painted and 'petroforms', if they consist of rocks and stones deliberately arranged to make a pattern.

Simply walking across the landscape with an observant and enquiring mind can lead to the discovery of archaeological features such as ditches, banks and mounds. There is a surprising amount of archaeology, known as 'above ground' archaeology, all around us that isn't buried and doesn't require

digging – field boundaries, crosses, boundary markers, early grave stones and rock art, for example. Studying these examples is a form of archaeology that is open to anyone to undertake – all the more so as it is non-invasive, and does little harm to the landscapes and objects being studied.

Reading the Landscape

One form of fieldwork is simply to go for a walk, known as 'a walkover', to explore and read the landscape, searching for remains that survive above the ground. These can be ancient earthworks, or 'humps and bumps', or they can be the evidence of more recent activity, such as canals, mills and mines.

Above Recording the lie of the land – its humps, bumps, ditches and furrows – is key to recognizing its archaeological potential.

Once bitten by the archaeology bug, life becomes one long field survey: whenever you travel, you'll habitually and instinctively scan the landscape for archaeological clues – whether walking to work through town, travelling by car or train or walking for exercise and leisure. With practice and familiarity, archaeologists learn to distinguish between features in the landscape that are natural and those that are the result of human intervention. It isn't easy, and some people have more of a gift than others. The changing seasons and, as we have already seen, varying times of day have an impact on what you see, as do different types of light and alternative states of vegetation. People who regularly find new sites tend to be those who have lived in an area for a long time, and who walk the same ground regularly.

Thinking you already know everything there is to learn about a street, building or landscape will never lead to new discoveries. You need to keep looking at the landscape with fresh eyes and asking questions, until one day, seen in a different light, something sings out that you haven't noticed before, such as an alignment of stones that looks deliberate rather than natural, or the slight scratches on a boulder that suddenly form a pattern when seen in the raking light of the winter sun, or the ditch that you suddenly realized was dug to divert water to some long vanished mill.

Systematic survey

You can do better than to make accidental discoveries: by selecting an area of the landscape and walking across it systematically, you can look

for evidence – or even record evidence that is staring you in the face but that nobody has recorded before. In many parts of Europe, for example, projects have been set up to record the fast-disappearing relics of twentieth-century warfare, from tank traps and gun emplacements hidden in woodland to decaying prisoner-of-war camps and gunpowder factories or the forgotten nuclear bunkers and rocket test sites of the Cold War.

Although there is a place for simply walking the landscape just to 'see what is there', patterns and meaning often do not emerge unless field survey is undertaken in a more systematic way. Some of the survey work undertaken by archaeologists is led by the desktop research they do, and is concerned, for example, with inspecting on the ground sites that they have found on aerial photographs. They may also plot the rise and fall of the land using electronic distance measurement (EDM) equipment. Three people are needed to operate the equipment, and this must be done in an area of open field with a clear view of the surroundings (*see opposite*). EDM is also used to plot excavated features during an actual dig, this is explained in part three (*see* Breaking New Ground).

Left The eroded banks of ditches and streams might also reveal buried remains, as can tracks and gates cut through banks or other earthworks – and long shadows.

Alternatively, you might set out to look for and compile maps of some very specific type of feature – books have recently been published on sheep pens and animal pounds, on medieval rabbit warrens and on water meadows and meadow management, all of which have resulted from systematic field survey work. In Northumberland, England, local volunteers have been scouring the upland moors for examples of prehistoric rock art, and they have added hundreds of new finds to the database of known examples.

In France an archaeologist on a walking holiday became fascinated with the boundary walls and marker stones, along with cairns (heaps of stone created by clearing the land for ploughing) that he noticed on the hills he was exploring. He returned later to study them using a systematic approach and has proved that they are the remains of intensive prehistoric agriculture on what is now a wild upland nature park.

Mole hills and cuttings

When you are out in the field, never miss the opportunity to examine disturbed ground. Countless sites have been discovered through nothing more sophisticated than the examination of soil thrown up by rabbits, moles, foxes, badgers and other ground-burrowing creatures. Archaeologists taking part in 'Time Team', the British television programme, discovered a splendid Roman villa with bath suite and mosaic floors after the landowner discovered the small stone cubes (tesserae) used by Roman mosaic makers in the soil turned up by moles burrowing in his field (*see* The Importance of Location).

However, the most common form of disturbance to buried archaeology has to be ploughing. The systematic walking of ploughed fields is an activity that is of huge importance to all archaeologists – but especially to local amateur societies, because it is one of the easiest and least expensive ways to contribute to archaeological knowledge, as well as to satisfy that thirst for new discovery that provides motivation for all archaeologists.

Conducting an earthworks survey using EDM

1 The reflector is fixed to a staff marked with a vertical scale, and is placed at the point where the ground rises or falls.

2 The EDM operator checks the spirit level to ensure the tripod is level, then looks through the lens at the reflector.

3 A small knob beside the lens adjusts the focus. The EDM then records the vertical and horizontal scale.

4 A third person then plots the distance on a graph, recording the rise and fall of the landscape.

Above Kenyan-based archaeologist Richard Leakey with one of the African fossils that has provided vital clues to early human history.

Looking for the first humans in Africa

Many a time, discoveries have been made in circumstances where someone less dedicated and less familiar with the terrain might have seen nothing. Richard and Maeve Leakey are well known for their systematic quest for fossil bones in Kenya. In August 1984, a member of the Leakey's survey team, Kamoya Kimeu, spotted a fragment of blackened bone, which was almost undistinguishable in colour from the surrounding black basalt pebbles of a dry river bed. However, he and the Leakeys were determined and continued searching the same spot for another four years. Their reward was to find numerous fragments of bone that eventually added up to the nearly complete skeleton of a teenager who lived 1.6 million years ago, now called 'the Turkana Boy' after nearby Lake Turkana.

The Importance of Location

Perhaps the most important piece of information that can be given about any archaeological site is its precise location. Any artefact taken out of the ground will lose the greater part of its archaeological value if there is no record of where it came from.

Above Recording location is crucial to placing a site within its wider historical context.

It is important to describe and analyse an archaeological site as fully as possible, but no single piece of information is quite so critical as saying where the site is, because that is the vital piece of data that allows other archaeologists to locate the site and study it further.

Location, location

To illustrate just how easy it is for sites to get lost, consider the subject of a UK 'Time Team' television programme, filmed in August 2005 at Withington, Gloucestershire. Withington is the site of a villa excavated in 1811 by the antiquarian, Samuel Lysons, after a ploughman discovered Roman remains in a field on which he was working. Excavations revealed some very fine mosaics (now in the British Museum), however no record was made at the time of exactly where the villa was

Left and below Archaeologists walking a site with a hand-held GPS (*left*) can import their track data – or 'waypoints' – into software such as Google Earth to produce a clear geographical profile. The Phoenecian port of Sabratha, Libya (*below*), was mapped in this way by Charlene Brown in 2006. Note that satellite maps are subject to continual updates.

located. Experts from 'Time Team' took two whole days before they managed to find it.

Location is also a very crucial piece of evidence in its own right, because it enables any one site to be located within a larger geographical context. As we have seen, the distribution of hill-forts, causewayed enclosures, temples, stone alignments or henges can tell us something about the influence of the people who built such monuments. The distribution of rock art in the landscape might give us clues about links between a certain rock-art pattern and ancient water sources, for example.

Pinpointing a site

For all these reasons, field survey work always begins by linking the area to be studied with a precise map location. This is easy enough at the macroscopic level — most of us can find where we live on a road map — but field work requires much greater precision.

Achieving that precision requires specialist surveying skills, though the principles are simple enough to understand. National mapping agencies have established certain fixed points on the earth's surface, known in different parts of the world as 'benchmarks', 'trig points', 'trigonometrical stations' or 'triangulation pillars'. These are points whose precise location has been measured in three dimensions — longitude, latitude and height above sea level. Starting from this known point, you can then work to the unknown

Above 'Benchmarks' are managed by the Ordnance Survey in the UK.

Above Using a total station needs clear and open terrain; woods and steep hills present real challenges to the surveyor.

point that you want to survey by using tape measures or surveying chains to measure distances, and you can use a special tripod-mounted optical instrument, called a theodolite, for measuring variations in height.

Similar equipment and techniques were used by the first map makers and the mathematical basis of surveying was understood by pyramid and temple builders in the distant past. Surveying by this method involves taking endless measurements and making a series of mathematical calculations. Over long distances, in difficult and overgrown terrain, mistakes are easily made, and yet skilled surveyors can plot precise locations with pinpoint accuracy.

The age of the GPS

All of this arcane knowledge is in the process of being made redundant with the advent of the Global Positioning System (GPS), a device that enables any point on the earth to be pinpointed by bouncing radio signals to a series of satellites orbiting the earth. There are many different types of GPS – from cheap hand-held devices that are accurate to within a metre or so, to large 'total stations', which have enough memory to store huge quantities of data in the field and are accurate to about 2mm (⅔sin).

Hand-held devices are useful for pinpointing the location of discrete monuments – a boulder with cup and ring marks, for example, or a standing stone. You can also use them to plot a

series of alignments – for example, tracing the locations of boundary marker stones or of a water course, irrigation canal or track.

The GPS is so easy to use that the biggest challenge now is to remember to carry spare batteries if you are working for long periods in the field – and even this problem can be overcome by using solar-powered equipment.

Total stations

Commercial units, surveyors and academic research groups use total stations to produce a terrain model. To do this involves first setting up a base station, whose position on the globe is located by satellite. An archaeologist wearing a backpack with an aerial and transmitter/receiver then walks across the site, guided by flags or poles set into the ground at intervals of 3–5m (10–16ft). The base station keeps a three-dimensional record of the entire walk, which can then be read by a computer and converted into graphic information. Usually this takes the form of a contoured plan of the site, accurate to within 3mm (⅛in) in the case of the most sophisticated systems. Thus, long hours (if not days) of surveying complex earthworks can now be reduced to a day of walking back and forth across the site, and the plotting of the results, which once also took several days, is now achieved using software that takes longer to print out than to process.

However, this system is not foolproof – dense woodland can defeat GPS signals, as can tall buildings – but having said that, surveying in such environments is challenging even when using conventional equipment.

Above The backpack worn by this archaeologist communicates with satellites in orbit around the earth to provide locational data with pinpoint accuracy.

Field Walking

The field survey techniques described so far have been concerned with understanding landscape use at a broad level. Having walked over a tract of landscape to identify sites of past activity, the next stage is to return to specific places for a closer examination of any surface finds.

Above The systematic inspection of land is an essential part of field survey.

The best time to do detailed field walking is after the site has been ploughed and after rain or frost has broken down the soil, which helps to wash out any archaeological material brought to the surface by cultivation. Mostly the finds exposed in this way will consist of fairly robust and durable materials – such as pottery, flint, building stone, brick or tile. Metal objects, such as nails or coins, might also be exposed, and these are best located using metal-detecting equipment (*see Metal Detecting*).

In an ideal world, this material should be left exactly where you find it, as a resource for other archaeologists to study. However, in reality it might be necessary to take the material away for adequate cleaning and analysis, so it follows that there are some important ground rules that archaeologists are expected to observe when they do this sort of work.

Know what is legal

First it is essential to check whether field walking is legal or not and obtain the necessary permits. In many European countries, the heritage is deemed to be publicly owned, and nobody is allowed to undertake archaeological work of any kind unless they have applied for and obtained a licence from the relevant state department. It is illegal almost everywhere in the world to take objects from protected monuments, and this can include sites that are designated for their wildlife and biodiversity as well as their archaeological value, since disturbing rocks and vegetation can have an impact on rare wildlife habitat.

Meet the landowner

In all circumstances, it is essential to gain the permission of the landowner for field walking, because, quite apart from the fact that it is common courtesy to do so, the landowner has a legal interest in any objects that are found on the land. Building a good relationship with the landowner can be vital to the success of a project in other ways, such as the timing of the work. You need the farmer to tell you when ploughing is going to take place, as the best time to sample ploughed fields is within the first three to four weeks after the soil has been turned, and before it has become compacted by heavy rain or by harrowing.

Few landowners object to non-intrusive archaeological activity on their land, if the purpose of the work is explained to them. On the contrary, many farmers have an intimate relationship with the land they cultivate, and they may have a deep and genuine

Left Field walking requires the co-operation of the landowner, so that crops are not harmed.

Protecting the land

The increasing power of farm machinery and more intensive agricultural practices mean that archaeological sites that have survived for many centuries are now being destroyed in a few short hours. Government agencies in Great Britain estimate that the landscape has been transformed by mechanized farming in the last 50 years, and that the landscapes known to our predecessors bore many more marks of past activity than the flat fields of today. The truth of this can be seen in landscapes used for army training on the Salisbury Plain, in central southern England, where, despite the destructive impact of tanks and explosives, there are thousands of above ground monuments within the Ministry of Defence estate, and almost none on adjoining properties which have been farmed.

Left Ancient field patterns and boundaries, which provide vital clues as to the archaeology beneath, can be destroyed when trees, hedges, banks and ditches are levelled to create a larger field for agricultural use.

interest in learning more about the people who were there before them. They often know the land better than anyone, and may be able to guide you toward areas where they have made finds in the past. They might also have maps and records relating to the history of the land and even, in some cases, a few bags or boxes full of the pottery they have found themselves. They can also prevent you from making embarrassing mistakes: archaeologists in Herefordshire, England, recently became excited by a large feature showing up on a geophysical scan, and were planning to investigate until the farmer told them that was where his father had buried a pile of rusty old wire some years previously.

Informing the landowner

Rather than demonize farmers for the destructive effects of ploughing, archaeologists try to prevent damage simply by telling farmers about the archaeology that can be found on their land. Although there are some farmers that are not interested, most are very happy to cease ploughing sensitive areas once they understand what lies beneath their soil. New grant regimes that reward farmers for sustainable farming and the protection of the historic environment are also beginning to have a beneficial effect on buried archaeology.

Above Few people understand the land so well as those who farm it. A farmer may be aware of fragments of pottery of other historic artefacts found on their land, and advise on where best to look for them.

Left Not all landscapes are easy to walk; searching for tell-tale signs in rocky or steep landscape requires skill and stamina.

Field Walking Techniques

Generally there are two stages to field walking: first, systematically walking across the ground in lines to identify where most of the material is located, then setting out grids to examine the most productive areas in more detail and determine the results of the field walk.

Above Ploughing turns over a 'sample' of what lies buried beneath farmed land.

By using a group of people walking carefully in lines, a large field can be surveyed fairly rapidly. Lines can be laid out at 15, 20 or 30m (50, 65 or 100ft) intervals, depending on how many people there are; however, at more than 30m (50ft), there is the risk of missing small scatters of material.

To ensure that people do not wander off line, ranging rods are used to mark out the walking lines. It is common practice to walk in a southerly to northerly direction across a field, simply because this aids plotting 'find' spots on a map (by convention, maps are always drawn with north at the top). The aim is to walk slowly along the line, scanning a metre or so along each side, looking for concentrations of finds lying on the surface of the ground, which are then marked using flags or poles. At this stage the aim is not to collect material so much as to identify where it is.

Grids and timing

The next stage is to examine the more productive areas in greater detail by dividing the site into squares. The size of the squares can vary from as small as 5 x 5m (16 x 16ft) to as large as 20 x 20m (65 x 65ft), depending on the scale of the site and the number of people involved. As the aim is not to collect absolutely everything, but rather to sample the site, larger squares are normally preferable.

The grids should be laid out on the ground using tapes, poles and strings, and they need to be plotted precisely on a base map, with each square given a unique number. Field walkers then spend a finite amount of time – perhaps 5 minutes for a small square and 15 minutes for a larger one – looking for surface finds in each square of the grid. Limiting the amount of time spent in each grid square is intended to counteract the fact that a field walker becomes much better at spotting objects the longer the patch of ground is studied. Tempting as it is to try and find every object within the grid, it is vital to move on to the next square once the allotted time is up to avoid bias information in favour of one square over another.

Team work

This work is usually done as a team effort, with some members doing the field walking, others identifying the finds and others recording them using a plan of the site and recording sheets.

At a very basic level, the finds from each grid should be sorted into basic types of material, such as worked flint, worked stone, shell, bone, brick, pottery, metal and so on. Each type of

Left A large area can be surveyed as part of a team effort, with everyone walking in straight lines at designated distances apart.

Right The finds from each area are bagged separately for later analysis: concentration of finds in one area might indicate a buried site.

Right The finds from each area are bagged separately for later analysis: concentration of finds in one area might indicate a buried site.

material is then counted and weighed, and the result is recorded on the site survey sheet, leaving the material itself behind where it was found. Done in this way, nothing is taken away from the site.

However, sometimes a find needs to be taken away for cleaning and further examination by an expert, so one member of the team will bag such finds and label them with the correct grid reference. The sorts of material that might be taken away include pottery and bone. In the case of pottery, the shape of the vessel, the decoration, the colour and the inclusions in the clay of the vessel can all be used by experts in dating the piece and assessing what the vessel might have been used for, whether it was for cooking, tableware or for the burial of cremated remains. In pieces of bone, experts will identify the type of animal, its age, the specific bone type and any butchery marks as evidence of farming practices, diet and ritual, refuse disposal or industrial processes, such as tanning.

Graphic results

The results can be presented graphically by using graded sized dots or by colour coding each grid, using a different colour for each artefact type and showing what percentage of each artefact type was found in the grid. The patterns that emerge from looking at the relative density of finds across a site can show where the activity was focused and, thus, where any buildings, pits or structures might be.

Concentrations of different materials can provide clues to the nature of the buried remains. For example, slag and burnt material might indicate an area of industrial activity, while tile and brick might indicate the location of a building; pottery might indicate a dwelling and large amounts of pottery of one type might suggest a warehouse or storage area. Animal bones or shell might indicate refuse pits, and large shards the waste from a kiln site.

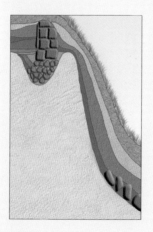

Above On hillsides, rain and soil 'creep' can carry material a long way.

Questioning the results

There are many reasons why finds should be treated with caution. One is the effect known as 'hill wash', where rain carries soil and the objects in it slowly downhill over many years. This can lead to an accumulation of material at the bottom of a slope, far away from the true settlement or activity site higher up the hill. Or it can lead to sites in the valley bottom becoming invisible – because the deposits are buried under a deep layer of soil, below the level of the plough. Some material can also arrive on site mixed up in manure from a farm or settlement some distance away – often the pottery that has arrived in this way is small and abraded, with rounded rather than sharp edges. So surface sampling is useful in helping to locate possible sites, but like all archaeological techniques, it often raises as many questions as it answers, and answering those questions involves further investigation, using electronic survey techniques that can look below ground and tell us what might be going on.

Metal Detecting

Metal detecting has often received bad press among archaeologists because inappropriate metal-detector use can cause irreversible harm. However, when used appropriately, metal detecting can make a valuable contribution toward archaeological techniques.

Above This copper harness decoration was unearthed during an excavation at Weedon Hill, Buckinghamshire, UK.

The chief accusations made against metal detectorists is that they can be unwilling to reveal the location of their finds in case other detectorists visit 'their' sites, and that they dig for 'treasure' rather than for knowledge, often destroying the contextual evidence that archaeologists need to reconstruct the past. Sometimes material is stolen from sites without being reported or given to the landowner, to whom it legally belongs, and there are particularly ruthless gangs of metal detectorists who raid monuments that are protected by law.

Reporting finds

To illustrate the loss of archaeological knowledge that can occur, imagine that a detectorist finds a bronze cup.

That vessel will have a monetary value, because there are people who collect antiquities and are willing to pay for good examples. However, the cup has no archaeological value unless a lot more is known about where it was buried, how it got into the soil and what else was buried with it.

In fact, something similar to this happened in March 2001 in the UK when Steve Bolger, a metal detectorist, discovered a beautiful Saxon drinking vessel. He reported the find even though he didn't have to (UK law requires only gold and silver finds to be reported: not bronze unless it is prehistoric), so archaeologists were able to visit the find spot and the subsequent excavation was captured on the UK television programme 'Time

Team'. The vessel was the merest hint of what lay beneath the soil. A rare and unusual Saxon cemetery dating from around AD 500, with bodies laid to rest along with their spears and shields, was subsequently uncovered.

Through further tests, archaeologists are hoping to find out where these people came from. This will help to fill the gaps in our knowledge about 'the Dark Ages', a name given to this period in European history because little is known about what happened at a time when Roman rule had collapsed and there were huge political and social upheavals in Europe, Africa and Asia.

The Nebra Sky Disc

Compare this with the equally true story of the spectacular Nebra Sky Disc – hailed as the world's oldest depiction of the cosmos. This circular bronze disc depicts the autumn sky, with crescent moon, sun and a cluster of stars – probably the Pleiades, or Seven Sisters, constellation. We now know that the disc was illegally excavated by metal detectorists in 1999 and sold several times before being seized by police in Switzerland, along with two metal-hilted swords dating from 1600 BC, which were found close to the disc. Because the detectorists gave misleading information about the find site, it took an enormous amount of detective work before police and archaeologists arrived at the place where the disk was found, at Nebra, in Saxony-Anhalt,

Left Underwater metal detectors prove extremely useful when surveying wrecks.

Below An Anglo-Saxon gold pendant is excavated with great care.

Above A metal dectectorist scans a mountain site for significant finds.

Codes of practice

In most countries, using a metal detector without a licence is illegal, yet the law is often ignored as there is no effective policing. Where it is allowed, the law requires you to obtain the landowner's permission and to operate within certain legal constraints. In Great Britain, for example, certain types of finds have to be reported to the District Coroner, including gold and silver objects, prehistoric metalwork and coins over 300 years old. For full details and The Metal Detecting Code of Practice visit the website of the Portable Antiquities Scheme, which is run by the British Museum:
• www.finds.org.uk/index.php
• www.finds.org.uk/documents/ CofP1.pdf
Another code of practice is available from English Heritage:
• www.english-heritage.org.uk/ upload/pdf/Our-Portable-Past.pdf
Information on metal detecting in the United States is available from the Federation of Metal Detector and Archaeological Clubs at:
• www.fmdac.org/

Germany. Excavation here led to the finding of a hilltop sanctuary, which is now thought to be an astronomical observatory, like Stonehenge.

Above Inlaid with gold and around 30cm (12in) in diameter, the spectacular bronze 'sky disc' of Nebra is the oldest known depiction of the heavens.

Common-sense guidelines

These are two contrasting examples of metal detecting: one involving naked theft of the heritage for personal gain and the other involving the responsible reporting of finds. In order to encourage more people to behave responsibly, archaeologists and metal detector clubs have drawn up codes of conduct that are full of common-sense guidance. The codes explain, for example, that permission must be gained in writing from the landowner before metal-detecting equipment is used. Detectorists are asked only to work on ground that has already been disturbed (such as ploughed land or land that has been ploughed in the past) and never to dig stratified archaeological deposits. Keeping an accurate record of finds and the spot where they were found is essential, and finds should always be reported to the local museum (in a perfect world, finds

should be donated to that museum, rather than sold for personal gain).

On the positive side, detectorists can also do a huge amount of good: dedicated metal-detector users who follow best practice guidelines have uncovered thousands of objects that might never have been known to archaeology. In Great Britain, more than 67,000 archaeological items and 427 pieces of treasure were discovered and reported by members of the public in 2005 alone. Some of the more spectacular examples, from Viking gold arm bands to medieval brooches, can be seen on the British Museum's Portable Antiquities Scheme website (*see box*).

Archaeological research

Of course, metal detecting also has a place within archaeological research. Most archaeologists now use metal detectors as part of surface sampling, simply because mud-coated metal

objects in ploughed soil are easy to miss when scanning by eye. For the same reason, metal detectors are used in excavations, to detect metal objects that diggers might miss when they clear soil from a site. It can also help locate buried metal so that a digger knows it is there in advance and can excavate it carefully to avoid accidental damage to the buried object.

Geophysical Surveys

'Geofizz' is the shorthand name for 'geophysical survey'. This involves using a battery of remote sensing devices linked to computers to show what lies beneath the soil. Geophysics is one of the most useful developments in archaeology of recent years.

Where once archaeologists had to guess at what lay under the soil from the evidence of aerial photographs and surface sampling, now they can use various devices that detect differences in the electrical or magnetic properties of features below the surface of the soil, provided it is not water-logged. As a result they know in advance not only where to dig, but also what they are likely to find. Drawing on clues from their research, archaeologists choose the most suitable method for that site.

Resistivity

One type of equipment is an electrical resistance meter, which has probes that measure higher or lower resistance to the flow of electricity. A stone wall, for example, impedes the flow and registers as an area of high resistance, whereas a pit or ditch conducts electricity more effectively and is registered as an area of low resistance.

These areas of higher and lower resistance are recorded as signals by the resistivity meter and can be converted,

Above A seismic survey can be used to detect the depth of buried features below ground.

using a computer programme, into a graphic image, showing areas of high (black or dark grey) and low (light grey to white) impedance. It is usually possible to interpret this pattern and see the clear outlines of buildings or ditches, but often it is only when the digging begins that it is possible to say what it is exactly that has produced the pattern of variations. There are plenty

Which type of geophysical survey equipment to use?

Above A resistivity meter records the levels of resistance encountered when a weak electrical current passes through the ground. Walls tend to resist current; pits and ditches show low resistance.

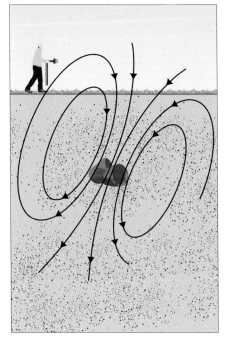

Above Magnetometry detects buried features whose magnetic field differs from the natural background field – often this is because the polarity has been altered through heat, so the technique is good for finding kilns and pottery.

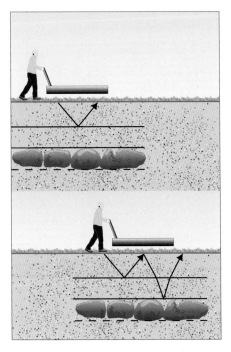

Above Ground-penetrating radar detects the speed with which radar signals bounce back when sent from the surface; the differences can be used to detect rock, soil, water, walls, pavements and voids.

of non-archaeological possibilities, ranging from buried pipes or electrical cables, to natural pockets of iron-rich soil or buried rubbish. Waterlogged soils are also difficult to survey because the ubiquity of such a good conductor of electricity swamps any minor fluctuations that might otherwise be detected from buried features.

For this reason, the technicians who specialize in geophysical survey are always guarded in their interpretation of the results. Scientifically, all that a resistivity survey can tell you is that there is an anomaly, in other words, something below the soil that is causing a pattern different to that of the normal electrical resistance properties of the soil. Even so, such surveys are very helpful in pinpointing precisely where the buried features are, and in showing areas that are empty of features.

Reistance meters are good at detecting solid features, such as the streets and buildings of a Roman town. This makes resistivity survey more useful to archaeologists dealing with classical sites in Italy, for example, and less so for those looking for the temporary camping sites of nomadic hunters.

Magnetometry

By contrast, the excavator of a camp site might gain better results from the use of a magnetometer. This measures the normal or natural magnetic field for the soil on the site being investigated. Sensors can then detect objects or areas below the soil that have a different polarity. That difference might indicate the presence of alien geology – for example, flints or worked stone with a stronger magnetic field than the background geology. Often it indicates areas of burning, which has the effect of fixing the direction of the magnetic field of the burnt earth at the place and time of the firing. Thus a hearth or a barbecue pit, or clay objects such as bricks or pottery, will show up as having a different magnetic field to the surrounding soil – and might thus indicate the presence below the soil of pits or ditches holding burnt material.

Great Britain's biggest geophysical survey

In 2002, the Landscape Research Centre completed work on a 220-ha (545-acre) geophysical survey of Yorkshire's Vale of Pickering, which involved members of the survey team walking an average of 10km (6 miles) a day, every day for two years. The results, plotted at a scale of 1:1000, filled a 3.5m- (11½ft-) long piece of paper. Geophysical survey was chosen because of the area's unusual geomorphology, with blown sand overlying buried archaeological deposits, preventing sites being visible as crop marks. The results showed that this 'empty' landscape was covered in archaeology, including Bronze Age tracks, dense Iron Age and Roman settlements, as well as Anglo-Saxon settlements and a cemetery.

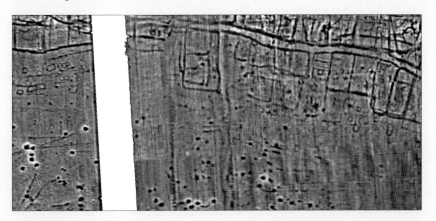

Above A geophysical survey at the Vale showed part of a Late Iron Age and Roman period 'ladder settlement', comprising a ditched trackway with a series of overlapping settlement enclosures at the top of the image, and distinctive sub-rectangular anomalies. These indicate the presence of Early Anglo-Saxon cavity floor buildings incorporating deep pits, designed to provide a dry air space beneath the floors of the buildings and invariably used as rubbish tips when they went out of use. The enhanced magnetic susceptibility of the discarded rubbish makes these features stand out quite distinctively in this type of survey.

However, there is one main deficiency of magnetometry – subtle differences in a magnetic field can easily be swamped by a large object or an object that is highly magnetic, or by one that is made of a metallic material that distorts the natural background polarity. This means that buried cables and metal pipes can make it impossible to conduct an accurate survey, as can a metal fence, a pylon or overhead electrical cables.

Ground penetrating radar

Because of the cost of the equipment, ground penetrating radar (GPR) is not as widely applied in archaeology as it is in oil prospecting, engineering or geological survey. The great advantage it has for archaeologists is in showing the depth of buried objects, adding the third dimension of depth to the two-dimensional plan view obtained from resistivity and magnetometry survey.

With GPR, a radar signal is sent into the ground, which bounces back to a receiver at different strengths and different time intervals. This signal is then converted to data about the solidity and nature of the soil and features within it. In some soils the results can be startlingly clear. Used in the uniformly sandy soils of a desert, small objects such as flint tools can be detected and pinpointed precisely. However, some types of subsoil such as clay are far less easy to penetrate than others and rocky soils scatter the signal, creating lots of meaningless feedback noise.

Geophysical Survey Methods

Geophysical surveys are now commonplace in archaeology because they are non-invasive (they produce useful data without destroying or harming the archaeology) and they enable large areas of ground to be surveyed at speed — at a fraction of the cost of stripping and excavating the same area.

Above A 'gradiometer' records magnetic variations to pinpoint buried archaeology.

The same basic methods are used to perform a geophysical survey, regardless of which type of equipment is being used (and the same basic approach also applies to field surveys, field walking and the use of metal detectors). Because survey techniques often produce better results when used in combination, archaeologists will usually deploy a whole battery of remote-sensing techniques combined

Below Seeing beneath the soil with a resistivity meter: following a grid line marked out with string, readings are taken at 1m (3ft) intervals.

with field walking when beginning their work of understanding a site (*see* Breaking New Ground).

The long walk

Doing a geophysical survey involves the somewhat tedious process of walking in straight lines backward and forward across the site, following guided tape measures and string lines that are set out in advance to mark out the survey area. In the case of resistivity or magnetometry equipment, the surveyor carries a pair of probes mounted on a frame. The probes are

inserted into the ground over and again at intervals of about one stride's length, or 1m (3ft), until the whole site is covered. One small site — say a suspected burial mound — might require the surveyor to walk up and down 100 times along a 50m (165ft) line, spaced at 1m (3ft) intervals — a

Above (top) Readings can be taken quickly and easily to log the position of features.

Above (bottom) Data logged by the resistivity meter is processed by computer to produce a map of buried ditches, pits and walls.

total of 5km (3 miles). With ground penetrating radar, the effort is not quite so demanding because the survey equipment is pulled across the ground on wheels.

Data analysis

The data that is captured by the survey instruments includes global positioning coordinates that pinpoint precisely where on the earth the readings were taken, plus the data from the ground, which then has to be interpreted. The data is transferred to a computer and converted, using specially designed software, into a series of contour lines, dots or grey-scale tones that are displayed on the screen or printed out.

The challenge is to interpret this pattern and understand what it is showing. This is where it is essential to be familiar with the shapes and patterns of typical archaeological sites and features. Identifying a Roman villa, for example, is relatively easy, but it takes skill and local knowledge to distinguish between a buried ditch and a buried bank, or between the circular ditch that surrounds a Bronze-Age burial mound and one of similar size surrounding an Iron-Age round house.

Often this is impossible unless you combine the data from a geophysical survey with finds from field walking or information from an aerial survey. Indeed, it is sometimes said that remote sensing works best if you already know what you are looking for! This is not as contradictory as it might sound. You might, for example, know from field walking that there is a kiln site somewhere in the vicinity, but not precisely where. Doing a geophysical survey will help to determine the exact location of an archaeological site that is known to exist.

Successes and failures

An example of the potentially misleading results of a geophysical survey comes from Leominster, Hereford-shire, where local archaeologists used ground penetrating radar (GPR) to investigate an area close to the town's historic priory church, which was due

Locating royal burials

In 2006 GPR was used with great success when archaeologists surveyed the floor of Edward the Confessor's Chapel at Westminster Abbey. The chapel was used as a mausoleum by the medieval kings and queens of England until the 14th century. GPR was deployed to locate graves, which could then be attributed to various members of the royal family by reference to medieval documents. Using GPR enabled this to be done without disturbing the splendid mosaic marble pavement that covers the chapel floor.

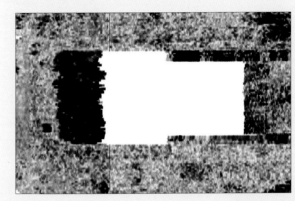

Left View of the shrine floor; image generated using ground-penetrating radar. These results show traces of a number of burials but the main image is the dark area – this is the packing used to seal the tomb entrance.

Right An image of a shipwreck was created from a sonar geophysical device. The data is collected as thousands of 'echo points'.

Below The torpedo-shaped echolocation device is known informally as a 'fish'.

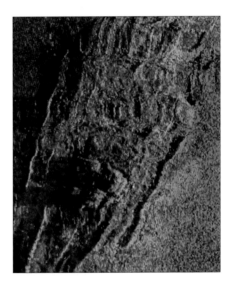

to be developed for use as a parking lot. The GPR survey revealed a circular structure beneath the soil that was the right shape and in the right position to be a baptistery. Excited archaeologists went into print in leading journals predicting the discovery of an important religious building. Sadly, it was not to be: when the soil was removed, the feature turned out to be a circular stone wall around flowerbeds and a flagpole built in the 1930s.

However, GPR was used rather more successfully at New York State's West Point Foundry, where only the

foundation walls survive. This is where railway engineers built the United States' first locomotive, dubbed *The Best Friend*. Although archaeologists knew that the machinery in the foundry was driven by a giant waterwheel, they were not able to locate the water channels that supplied the wheel. Rather than excavating large areas, ground pene-trating radar (GPR) was used to search for the channels, which led them to the buried pipework and stone lined culverts that underlie the cobbled foundry floor. They were able to find the source and preserve the floor.

The Message in the Hedges

Not all archaeological survey techniques involve high-tech equipment: some archaeologists use hedges and vegetation as a clue to the way that the landscape was used in the past. Hedge survey is one of the more intriguing developments in archaeology in recent decades.

Above Hawthorn is quick growing and much used in modern hedges.

In the 1970s amateur and professional archaeologists expressed great excitement when claims were made that a simple dating formula had been created based on counting species. According to this theory, all you had to do was count the woodland tree species in a 91.5-m (100-yd) stretch of hedge, and each species was said to represent an additional 100 years in the age of the hedge. This means that a species-rich hedge with a mix of elm, oak, blackthorn, hawthorn, holly, ash,

willow, wild pear, elderflower and field maple might be a 1,000-year-old Saxon hedge, whereas a hawthorn hedge with few other species is likely to have been planted more recently during the 19th or 20th centuries.

Woodland origins

The assumption behind this formula was that older hedges started out as woodland, however, bit by bit the timber from the wood was cleared, leaving a new field bound by such trees

as the farmer chose to leave as a cattle barrier or property line. There was another theory, which held that the hedges gained species through time as wind-born or bird-born seeds became trapped by the hedge, germinated, grew and seeded to become an established part of the matrix.

Of course, nothing in life is ever that simple, and hedge specialists working in Norfolk, Shropshire and Northumbria have now concluded, after studying thousands of miles of hedge, that the truth to the origins of a species-rich hedge is more complex and more interesting than the 100-year formula suggests. (For more in-depth coverage of the subject, see *Hedgerow History: Ecology, History and Landscape Character* by Gerry Barnes and Tom Williamson).

Challenging assumptions

Long-established hedges were often replanted and realigned in the 18th and 19th centuries to conform more closely to the ideals of agricultural improvers – crooked hedges were straightened and ancient hedges with large timbers or mature trees were cropped and replaced by quickthorn. Diaries and farm records show that species-rich hedges can be very recent, because farmers used the local woods as a source for hedging material, taking seedlings of any variety they could find. Archdeacon Plymley, writing in the 18th century, wrote, for example: 'I enclosed a small common...a trench

Above The lush landscape of the Arenal region, Costa Rica, has been subject to intensive aerial and ground survey.

Tracing ancient footpaths

Satellite imaging has recently been used to spot changes in vegetation that indicate the routes of 2,000-year-old processional pathways. They are in the Arenal region of present-day Costa Rica, and are invisible to observers on the ground. The repeated use of these paths to navigate rugged terrain between small villages and ancestral cemeteries over several centuries created shallow trenches, which now collect moisture. The lusher growth produced by vegetation in response to the extra water can be detected in infrared satellite photography, even in places where thick vegetation prevents archaeologists from treading today, or where the trenches are now hidden after being filled in by layers of ash from prehistoric volcanic eruptions.

Since studying these processional routes, archaeologists have found pottery that suggests they were used for more than 1,000 years, from roughly 500BC to AD600. People returned to them year after year for ritual feasts, despite abandoning their villages because of eruptions from the nearby Arenal Volcano.

Above When excavating historic buildings, such as farmhouses, archaeologists pay close attention to the vegetation of the site.

was dug of considerable width and depth. Strong bushes of hazel, willow, hawthorn or whatever could be met with in a neighbouring wood, were planted in this trench…young hawthorns or hollies or their berries, were [then] put between the stems.'

However, although archaeologists have to treat the results of hedge survey with some caution, they don't have to throw hedge study out of their toolbox altogether. If a combination of indicators are found – multiple species, sinuous hedges, planted on a bank, perhaps beside a sunken lane, and perhaps also forming the boundary of a parish or farm – the accumulation of detail begins to suggest that the hedge, or its ancestors, have been around for some time. Studies in France, Germany and the Netherlands suggest that the hedges used to separate fields from lanes are typically 700 years old, and the word 'hedge' itself is derived from the Anglo Saxon word *hecg* (*hecke* in Old German, *haag* in Dutch).

Revelations from plants

In recent years, archaeologists have also begun to pay close attention to the types of plants growing on ancient sites and on the differences in vegetation density. Using geochemical analysis, they have discovered that where animals have been kept or where manure – of human or animal origin – has been stored or deliberately buried, chemicals in the soil encourage taller growth of plants that like a high phosphate level, such as nettles. This effect can persist not for years or decades but for centuries. On medieval village sites, for example, this phenomenon has been used to distinguish between houses built for humans and byres for cattle; or to determine which end of a longhouse the humans lived in and which end housed the animals.

Some plants, by contrast, favour very thin, poor soils, where they thrive because of the lack of competition from more vigorous competitors.

Above Nettles with nitrogen-rich disturbed soil and dense growth often indicate places where animals have been fed in the past.

Clover is one such plant, and in summer, when the clover is more obvious because it is in flower, it is possible to survey buried walls and solid features simply by looking for the lines of white clover flowers.

Below Woods rich in hazel were once planted to provide timber for fences, baskets and thatching materials.

Above Slow-growing holly is often found in older hedges: in folklore, the prickly leaves were said to guard property from evil spirits.

Case Study: Survey at Portus Romae

The British and Italian archaeologists who studied Portus Romae, the ancient port of imperial Rome, set out with the deliberate intention of seeing how much information they could gather without doing any excavation — they were met with great success.

Above Reconstruction of warehouse fronts at Portus, where shipped goods were stored.

Passengers flying into Rome's Fiumicino Airport might be forgiven for thinking that the lake they can see from the left-hand side of the aeroplane, just south of the runway on the northern bank of the River Tiber, is a natural salt-water lagoon of the type that is very common along this stretch of the Italian coast. However, if they look again they will see that it is actually hexagonal (with six straight sides) in shape.

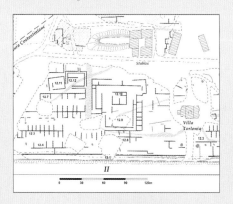

Evidence found in a name and location

This unnatural shape, spotted on maps and aerial photographs, alerted the archaeologists to the presence of something unusual at the mouth of the Tiber, and placename research revealed that it was known as Portus – Latin for 'door' or 'gateway', but also the word for a harbour that has given us the English word 'port'.

Searching through archives revealed that excavations had taken place in 1867/8, in the 1930s and again in the 1960s. These revealed that Emperor Claudius (who ruled from AD41–54) had built an offshore harbour at the

Left and below Magnetometer survey evidence for the location of the temple and warehouses at Portus (*below*), with magnetic anomalies appearing as solid dark lines. The drawn plan (*left*) interprets this data, plotting the location and possible structure of these buried features.

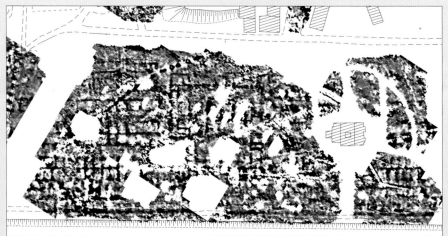

Tiber mouth, but as Rome grew it proved to be too small to cope with the volume of shipping bringing grain and oil from various parts of the Empire, especially from North Africa, to feed the citizens of Rome. One of Cladius's successors, Emperor Trajan (AD98–117), built the huge hexagonal inner harbour, which is 700m (3,000ft) across, with sides of 358m (1,175ft) in length. In doing so, Trajan did what Rome had done on other occasions and borrowed ideas from its bitter enemy, the Carthaginians – the source of the hexagonal form of the inland port.

Discovering a large port complex

Previous excavations had looked at only a fraction of the site, so geophysical survey techniques were used to see just how much else remained below ground. Magnetometry was used as the primary survey technique because this can generally be undertaken more rapidly. Resistivity was also deployed to explore areas of particular interest or uncertainty.

The magnetometer survey revealed that the port complex was a massive 1,000ha (2,470 acres) in extent. The survey also led to several major new discoveries. One of these finds was the existence of a large canal 40m (130ft) wide linking the hexagonal harbour to the River Tiber. The survey team also discovered the buried remains of a large and imposing columned building placed where it would be clearly visible to every ship entering the port. A suggestion is that perhaps the building was a temple, which might have been fronted by a statue of the emperor, emphasizing to travellers from the far-flung corners of the Empire that they had now arrived in the capital, Rome.

A massive sorting task

Scores of structures were located by the magnetometer survey, and they were all associated with the bustling public, commercial and industrial life of the harbour, so the team used field walking to try and sort out which buildings were used for what purpose. A huge quantity of pottery, tile, brick and iron had been brought up to the surface by ploughing, and the sheer amount of material that needed to be weighed and measured presented the archaeologists with a major task, but it proved to be an effective way of allowing significant patterns and differences to emerge.

The pottery and building materials collected by the survey team were sorted by class into fine tablewares, coarser cooking and storage wares and amphorae – the distinctive tall two-handled jars used by the Romans for transporting oil, wine, olives and fish sauce – and the building materials were sorted by function into roof tiles, brick, floor tiles, column fragments, and so on. The relative densities of these different materials across the site were then mapped by computer.

This enabled the team to guess which buildings might have been warehouses (large quantities of amphorae used as storage jars), which might have been industrial complexes (large quantities of iron slag) and which ones might have been grain warehouses (almost no finds), shops (a wide variety of different types of pottery) or offices and customs buildings (cubes of tesserae from mosaic floors). Some buildings produced lots of marble

Right Hypothetical computer reconstruction of late 2nd century AD warehouses (Grande Magazzini di Settimio Severo) at Portus.

Reconstructing the development of Portus

Right The Port of Claudius originated in the 1st century AD. Connected to the River Tiber by canals, it was an unusual choice of location due to poor shelter and a tendency to silt up.

Below The distinctive hexagonal pool (*below right*) took shape during the reign of Trajan (98–117BC). It had good storage capacity and was lined with warehouses. The later antique port (*below*), which survived until the 6th century AD, remained fortified, although building activity had slackened by this period.

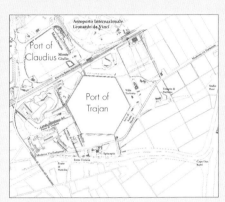

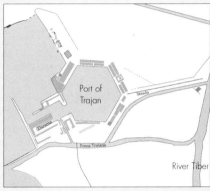

fragments, suggesting that raw marble was shipped to Portus from elsewhere, turned into columns and other architectural elements on site, then shipped up river to Rome.

A thriving trading centre

Looking at the origin of the pottery found on site, it was clear that most of the imports shipped into Portus and bound for Rome came from Africa and the eastern Mediterranean. Dating of the finds revealed a further surprise:

it was evident that the port continued in use at least into the early 7th century. This ties up with the historical evidence for Portus as the seat of a bishopric in the 4th century, granted municipal status under the Emperor Constantine, when the Basilica of Sant' Ippolito was built on the site. And if Portus was thriving then, perhaps Rome – the imperial capital – was thriving, too, despite the picture of barbarian attack and sacking that has come down to us from history.

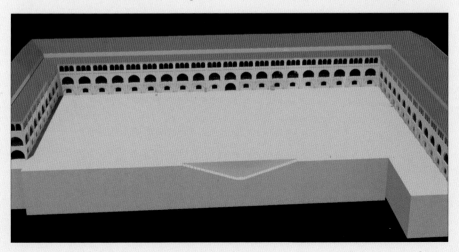

BREAKING NEW GROUND

The moment that an archaeologist puts a spade into the ground and begins to dig, he or she enters into a whole series of professional and academic obligations – to dig scientifically, to record accurately what is found, to treat all the archaeology with equal respect (rather than, as in the past, disregarding recent material in favour of Roman, for example), to make proper arrangements for the conservation, study and future storage of all the finds, to publish a record of what was found and to make provision for archiving the results of the excavation so that future archaeologists have access to them. To this onerous list, add another of health and safety responsibilities and legal obligations. Yet, there is still the sheer excitement of digging, and the sense of embarking on a voyage of discovery. No matter how thoroughly the desktop analysis was done that precedes the excavation, it is almost always the case that there is more below the ground than anyone predicted.

Opposite Archaeologists use small trowels to excavate the boundary wall to a historic harbour site.

Above The earth is delicately prised away from two skulls lying in situ in a burial site.

Above An archaeology student practises trowelling techniques during a research excavation.

Above Unravelling the history of this Roman site requires careful excavation and observation.

Excavation Strategies

Archaeology is complex, so it is not surprising that there is not one simple method of digging. There are many excavation strategies, some or all of which might be used on a site. The differences between rescue and research-led archaeology can account for the way in which a site is excavated.

As mentioned earlier, development-led 'rescue' archaeology is performed in response to the imminent destruction of archaeological remains that are being threatened by new development. This means that development-led archaeologists are more constrained than research archaeologists – the site of the excavation is not one that they have chosen to investigate to answer research questions, but one that has been dictated by the planning and development process. They have very little time to rescue any archaeology that may be present.

By contrast, research archaeology is elective – it is something chosen to answer important questions that can only be answered through excavating a particular site that has been identified as capable of yielding those answers.

Engineering solutions

Developers do everything they can to avoid the costs involved in large-scale excavation, and archaeologists have a similar desire to dig only as much as is absolutely necessary, because of the destructive nature of archaeology. Working together, developers and archaeologists aim to design buildings and structures that will avoid harming the archaeology.

One way to do this is by simply avoiding the archaeology. If the planned route of a gas pipeline is heading straight for a field that looks, from aerial photography, as if it contains a prehistoric enclosure, every effort will be made to change the pipeline route. On an urban development site, engineers will try to place the piles and foundations needed to support the new

Above If topsoil has previously been disturbed it can be removed by a mechanical digger.

building well away from archaeologically sensitive areas. One common strategy is to build a raft of recycled concrete over the top of the archaeological remains and build on top of the raft, without disturbing the soil below. Another is to use 'flying foundations', which are designed to carry the weight of the building on relatively slender piles that only disturb, say, 10 per cent of the buried archaeology rather than 25 per cent.

Preservation *in situ*

One strategy is known in the archaeological trade by the acronym PARIS, for 'Preserving ARchaeology *In Situ*' – *in situ* being Latin for 'in place', or 'not removed'. It aims to preserve as much archaeology as possible in the place and in the state in which it was originally formed or deposited. However, because it is rarely possible to leave 100 per cent of the archaeology *in situ*, archaeologists often deal with various situations where very small areas of the site are excavated – using techniques that are often described as 'keyhole archaeology'.

Keyhole archaeology

A 'watching brief' might be one part of keyhole archaeology. It involves being on site as engineers dig foundation trenches or drill piles into the soil, to

Left At their most successful, test pits function as a small-scale excavation, presenting a microcosm of the whole site.

Right An archaeologist watches as heavy machinery opens a trench for inspection. He has marked the traces of a feature in the soil and must monitor digging carefully.

see if anything archaeological turns up in the excavated soil. Watching briefs are only used in circumstances where prior desktop research suggests there isn't any archaeology; in other words it is a back-up strategy. In theory, if the excavating machinery starts to produce archaeological remains, engineering work can stop while a proper investigation is carried out. In practice, it is often very difficult to interpret the odd finds that might emerge in the bucket of a digger, no matter how carefully the digger driver tries to be, so this is a ham-fisted form of excavation compared with the precision of a trowel wielded by an experienced archaeologist.

Test pits

Preferable to a watching brief is the opportunity to sink test pits or trial trenches into the ground, targeting the areas that will be destroyed in later construction work, such as the areas where piles are to be sunk. Yet this can be a frustrating type of archaeology, too, because small-scale excavation nearly always raises more questions than it answers. Imagine trying to understand the picture depicted in a complex jigsaw when you only have a few small pieces to go on. The problem with both test pits and trial trenches is that, however carefully they are sited, they might miss significant parts of the archaeology. One example occurred when the Eton Rowing Lake was excavated at Dorney, along the River Thames near Windsor in southern England. Numerous trial trenches missed an enormous deposit of worked Neolithic flint that was found once the engineering work began.

However, test pits do have a value. They can be used to examine the nature and extent of any archaeological remains, and to make judgements about whether further large-scale excavation is needed.

Research excavation

Although rescue and research-led excavation techniques are not mutually exclusive, there are often important differences in how an excavation proceeds. The director of a research excavation is less constrained in terms of time or the choice of technique, and the placing of trenches can be dictated by the nature of the archaeology and the questions that are being asked, rather than by engineering decisions about where to place shafts, piles or trenches for service pipes.

The research archaeologist is often in the fortunate position of being able to plan several seasons of work at one site, and the time between one season and the next can be used as important thinking time, during which finds can be analysed and excavation aims modified in the light of feedback from specialists. In commercial work, the tight time constraints that apply on a building site demand fast work by the archaeologist and little time for second thoughts or to go back and rethink any interpretations.

Rescuing London's heritage

Preservation in situ normally means preserving archaeological remains without excavating them, on the basis that it is better to preserve than to destroy. Sometimes it can also mean excavating the remains and then preserving what was found, rather than, as often happens, digging a big hole and taking away all the archaeology to allow an underground parking lot or plant room to be built.

In 1988, Museum of London archaeologists made an unexpected discovery in London when they unearthed the city's Roman amphitheatre on the site of a new art gallery. These

Above Excavating a Roman timber box from a drain during the rescue excavation at London's buried Roman amphitheatre.

2,000-year-old remains were so important that the site was declared a protected monument, and the masonry of the amphitheatre was incorporated into the design of the art gallery's basement, where it is now a popular visitor attraction.

Large-scale Excavation

The most satisfying archaeology, and the most rewarding, is the excavation of a large area, so that a part of the landscape can be investigated in its entirety, leading to an understanding of continuity and change over time. This can occur in both development-led and research-led archaeology.

Sometimes, the scale of development is so large that substantial resources are allocated to a project, enabling work to be done that is the envy of research-based archaeologists. This is especially the case when the developer wants to be seen as acting responsibly toward the natural and historic environment and goes beyond the minimum that is legally required, giving archaeologists the money and time to do the best possible job.

This has been the case in England, for example, with the construction of new industrial, commercial and housing estates around the new town of Peterborough, and in the Cotswold Water Park, where huge areas of countryside have been excavated for sand and gravel. Within cities, the equivalent is the development of a whole block, involving deep excavations, as occurred in London during the construction of new underground stations on the Jubilee Line, or in Istanbul, during the construction of a new railway tunnel beneath the Bosporus, linking Europe and Asia.

Total archaeology

Excavations of large areas are at the extreme end of the archaeological scale and are extremely expensive to mount, not just because of the costs of hiring skilled people and all the necessary equipment, but because the excavation costs typically amount to only 40 per cent of the total cost of the project. Post-excavation costs – for conserving and studying all the material found during excavation, and for publishing and archiving the results – account for the balance, and these can be considerably higher if the results are so important that a decision is made to fund a permanent visitor centre or museum on the site.

Total excavation is, therefore, rare. It is often the case that such archaeology is funded by public utilities or govern-

Above Large-scale excavation may involve dividing a site, such as the ancient farm shown above, into several smaller sub-sites.

mental bodies as part of the infra-structural cost of achieving a publicly desirable objective such as new transport systems, pipelines, Olympic facilities or mineral extraction.

Putting things into context

Where such opportunities occur, they offer an important counterbalance to small-scale excavation, which gives in-depth information about a particular site. From the information gained during a small-scale excavation, archaeologists try to develop general theories that apply to all monuments of that type. So excavating one Romano-British farmstead, for example, can provide data about the accommodation for humans and animals, field size and number, crops grown and storage methods, whether the farm was self-sufficient or involved in specialized production for trade, how and when the farm was founded, evolved and was abandoned, and what changes occurred during the period that it was in use. (*For a case-study example, see Frocester Court.*)

Large-scale archaeology can then put this information into context and reveal patterns at the level of a whole landscape. Is the Romano-British farmstead typical or unusual, what came before and after, what can be learnt about the use of the landscape over a long period of time, does the

Left A rescue excavation in progress at the heart of a large shopping complex.

Right Excavations at the site of London Heathrow Airport's Terminal 5 revealed the straight line of Roman field ditches and the post pits of a prehistoric timber monument.

pattern revealed by the landscape suggest slow steady continuity of people and culture, and are there distinct episodes of change and innovation, war and conquest, culture succeeding culture?

Excavation at Heathrow

The site of London Heathrow Airport's Terminal 5 building was the location for one of Great Britain's largest-ever excavations. The site, over 100ha (250 acres), took 18 months to investigate and the story that emerged perhaps represents the potted history of a large part of England.

The first evidence of human activity in the heavily forested landscape of 8,000 years ago (the Mesolithic, or Middle Stone Age) consists of cooking pits that were visited again and again and used for many generations – evidence, perhaps, of regular ritual gatherings. Bigger monuments were then constructed in the Neolithic period (4000–3600BC), consisting of rows of posts and long ditches and banks, built in such a way as to suggest that the builders were aware of the older pits and wished to incorporate them into their own structures.

These monuments continued in use for hundreds of years as people slowly cleared the woodland landscape, creating fields and permanent settlements, with trackways, houses, food storage pits and waterholes. Before this, land was probably shared by the whole community, but with settlement came the first boundaries (ditches and banks with hedges or timber palisades) dating from 2000BC (the Early Bronze Age), which show that people were claiming ownership of specific areas of land for the first time.

Right In a classic rescue project, a Christian funeral basilica from the 5th century AD was excavated in 2004 in Marseille, France, prior to the construction of a parking lot on the site.

Above After stripping the topsoil by machine, more delicate excavation begins.

Above On such large sites as Heathrow, digital recording comes to the fore.

In the Middle Bronze Age (1500–1100BC), landholdings begin to consolidate into fewer but larger settlements. This process of nucleation continues through the early Iron Age (from 700BC), when there are only two settlements. By the time of the Roman conquest, there was just one large settlement at the centre of the block. From this period into the Roman period, there was no fundamental change to the architecture of the landscape. New land divisions respect older monuments and there is no sense that the past was forgotten or ignored, until the 3rd century AD, when a ladder-like field system was imposed on the landscape without reference to anything that had been before. The Romans simply transformed the world they found and made it new, but only after two centuries of occupation. Their field systems and settlements lasted only a short time. The village of the Roman era died out and was replaced by a new village in the 12th century.

Setting up a Research Project

Keyhole archaeology and total excavation represent the extremes of archaeological practice, but most excavations lie in the middle ground. Here is a more typical approach to how a research project is set up, staffed by a mix of experienced archaeologists and students, trainees and volunteers.

Above These archaeologists are setting up an excavation site in Kazakhstan.

The logistics involved in setting up an excavation are very complex, and television programmes based on the idea that archaeological problems can be resolved in a long weekend are misleading. Those programmes actually involve many weeks of preparation work beforehand, involving a team of producers employed on a regular basis, and they often show only a small part of what is, in reality, a much longer programme of archaeological research.

Before digging begins

Digs are usually run by a director (often with one or more deputies to share the load). The first task facing the director of a research-based excavation is to gain permission to dig. Legal constraints and property laws mean that you cannot simply dig at will. In many countries, a licence to excavate is required, especially if the site to be investigated is legally classified as a protected monument. Gaining a licence often involves a great deal of previous research to convince the relevant state heritage authorities that excavation really is necessary, because the site is under threat or because digging is the only way to answer key research questions.

As well as undertaking a very thorough desktop assessment and proving that the site fits established and agreed research strategies, a common tactic is to form a project steering group and invite fellow researchers to act as advisers to the project. That way they can validate your work, act as referees and vouch for the value and necessity of the work. The same experts might also agree to be part of the post-excavation team, providing invaluable expertise in identifying and analysing the finds.

The end result of this initial process is a formal document known as a 'Project Design', which sets out clearly what is known about the site, why excavation is justified, what the aims of the excavation are and what contribution will be made to the knowledge of the past through excavation of the site.

Paying the bills

Another essential and time-consuming task is ensuring that the costs of the excavation are planned for and that funding is in place to meet all the expenses. Excavations are often funded by a mosaic of small grants from archaeological societies, charitable trusts, donations and sponsorship. Or they might be funded by academic institutions, learned societies and research academies, such as the internationals schools of archaeology maintained by various governments in parts of the world that are the major

Left The ongoing Tayinat Archaeological Project, abbreviated to TAP, is an initiative by the University of Toronto to chart the rise of urban civilizations in ancient Turkey.

Right University students will sometimes work in pairs on a research dig, one to excavate and the other to record what is found.

focus for archaeological research. (The UK, German, United States, Swiss, Norwegian, Dutch and Finnish governments all have research schools in Rome, Athens, Ankara, Nairobi, Tehran, Amman and Jerusalem.) Once again, this is where forward planning is essential, because grant applications have to be made months in advance of the dig and approaches need to be made well in advance to potential donors of equipment and money.

Multi-tasking skills

The director has to be a person of many skills, because while research and financial management abilities are essential to the dig's viability, there are many mundane tasks to attend to as well. When will the dig take place? If the dig depends on volunteers, then it has to take place at a time when volunteers are available, and that usually means timing it for university holiday periods. In fact much research archaeology takes place in the summer for this reason.

How many people are needed and how will they be recruited? Students of archaeology form the backbone of the workforce, simply because it is a requirement of many university courses that students spend a minimum period of time gaining fieldwork experience. This core workforce can be augmented by volunteers from the community, including members of a local archaeology society.

In either case, the excavation might be advertised months ahead in archaeological magazines and websites. Before advertising the excavation, key decisions have to be made about how long will be needed for the dig to take place, the number of people required and their skill levels, and where the diggers will be accommodated and fed and how much they will be charged. The fees that participants pay for training and daily sustenance are a vital part of the business plan for any dig.

Human resources

Typically, a research dig will take place over a 4- to 6-week period, employing a workforce of 30 people or more. Some excavations provide accommodation and food, while others may provide no more than a campsite and a water supply.

If that sounds rather bohemian, it is often the case that digs can be very memorable experiences that live in people's memories for the rest of their lives. Working as a member of a team on a project that might be located in a beautiful part of the countryside, often with good weather (possibly also with excellent local food) and involving a mix of physical and intellectual challenges is a powerful formula for enticing participants. The social side of

Above With large numbers of people on a project, briefing meetings are essential. These are held on a regular basis during excavation – usually at the start and/or close of the day.

an excavation also plays an important role (which is one reason why archaeologists who dig together often become close friends).

A participant might find him or herself working as part of a multi-cultural, multinational team, working in a part of the world where he or she becomes part of the local community for a period of time. Even if a participant is not planning to become a professional archaeologist, going on a dig is an excellent way to get close to other cultures and meet people from other backgrounds.

The Tools for the Job

Having sorted out the human and financial resources, the next task a director faces is that of bringing together the many tools that are needed on an average excavation. The precise list of tools and equipment will depend on the scale, character and duration of the dig.

Even a small simple excavation that needs only the basic resources can require a long checklist of equipment. To start with, there is the equipment used for doing the actual digging, string, nails and tape measures for marking out the trenches, a turfing tool for cutting and skimming off the turf, and spades, picks and shovels for moving earth. On top of that the digging process will call for brushes, hand shovels, buckets, the wheel-barrow and planks used for taking the excavated soil away from the site for wet and dry sieving (sifting) and for building a safe spoil tip (heap).

As the site begins to yield archaeo-logical material, waterproof labels and pens will be necessary for labelling finds and soil changes, and bags will be required for storing finds and soil samples. Every find and soil type has to be recorded using previously prepared record sheets. Further detailed records of the site might also need to be captured, and this can involve using a camera and drawing plans and sections using grids, graph paper, tape measures and pencils.

The digger's pride and joy

Most of the tools used in archaeology can be acquired from other people's toolkits – the builder, surveyor, gardener or artist. However, there is one tool that is distinctively archaeo-logical: the trowel. This has to be a special sort of trowel, not the curved

Above The ubiquitous trowel is the key tool in an archaeologist's fieldwork kit. Seasoned archaeologists may carry more than one, choosing the best tool for the job in hand.

type used by gardeners or the large flat trowels preferred by bricklayers, masons or plasterers. Working with archaeologists over many years, the British tool manufacturer Spear & Jackson has developed a specially designed tool, called the WHS (named after the tool's original manufacturers, William Hunt & Sons), that is forged from steel with a 10cm (4in) blade and a comfortable rubber handle and finger guard.

However, as with all things, trowel preferences can be cultural: while British archaeologists favour the WHS model, many mainland European archaeologists prefer the slightly shorter and broader Italian-made Battiferro pointing trowel. In North America, the slightly longer 11.4cm (4½in) Marshalltown pointing trowel is the preferred choice of many archaeologists, and though it might be much more expensive than its European counterparts, it does come with its own belt holster, so there is less risk of putting it down somewhere and forgetting where.

Trowels have many functions. Used as a blade, lever and scraper, trowels represent the archaeological equivalent

Left The volunteer archaeologist is likely to encounter a selection of tools, including creature comforts such as a thermal flask or sun hat to plastic ties for 'bagging and tagging' archaeological finds.

Sun hat and water bottle to prevent dehydration

Tape measure for drawing plans

String for marking out the edges of a site

Trowels

Plasterer's leaf

Metal pegs for securing labels and string lines

Plastic ties for securing bags

Gloves to prevent blisters

Dental toothpick for delicate excavation

The purpose of test pits

Prior to opening up the main part of a site, the director might use test pits, measuring 1 x 1m (3 x 3ft), as a training exercise to familiarize the diggers with the soil conditions and the nature of the local geology. Test pits can also be used to investigate how deep the deposits are, or how well preserved they are – especially in fields that might have been ploughed or in soils that corrode bone or organic remains. Test pitting can help a director decide whether the topsoil contains archaeological material and needs to be excavated by hand, or whether it is so disturbed that machine excavation can be used. Another common practice is to dig a sequence of test pits across a site or around the perimeter to find out just how far the site extends; for example, to see whether there are any burials outside a cemetery wall or enclosure ditch.

Left A small area of turf and topsoil are removed to create a test pit. The content of the pit, which is recorded, may affect the decision on how and where to dig.

of the surgeon's scalpel, used for precise and delicate tasks on site. However, they can also perform all the tasks that are involved in excavating and cleaning archaeological features. On some types of excavation site, where absolute precision is needed to preserve the finds, trowels are the only 'large' tool permitted on site, along with plastic scrapers, dental tools and even modified cutlery.

Trowel etiquette

Whatever the model, size or shape of the trowel when it is new, the trowel will change shape and size over time, especially if it has been used over time for digging abrasive surfaces, such as stone. Seasoned archaeologists usually carry their trowels with pride: wear and tear is seen as a symbol of experience and prowess, and each trowel, once worn, has its own character. In fact, some archaeologists often carry more than one trowel and will select a different tool for fairly robust work and another for the precision needed to excavate bones or metalwork, or complete pots.

Because trowels are so personal, archaeologists are fiercely protective of them. It is very much a taboo to borrow someone's trowel – and certainly not without the owner's express permission, so bear this in mind if you are working on a site for the first time.

Large machinery

Archaeologists are equally willing to use large machinery on sites. Once you have ascertained, usually by test pits or trial trenches, that there is nothing of archaeological value in the topsoil, this can be cleared from the site by bringing in a tractor with scraper bucket or back hoe. Pneumatic hammers are often necessary to break through concrete floors or other solid obstructions on urban sites.

Needless to say, the use of such heavy equipment is expensive, requires trained operators and has health and

Above Earth-moving machinery is carefully monitored by archaeologists and camera crew at a live televised dig, Windsor Castle, England.

safety and insurance implications, but such costs have to be weighed against the time saved in opening up the site and getting down to the real task in hand. Some archaeologists even provide a specialist contracting service and will undertake this kind of work with delicacy and skill, and an understanding of archaeological objectives that might be missing in a general contractor.

Risk Assessment and Security

The director's list of pre-excavation tasks is not finished yet: archaeological excavation also involves a whole additional set of management and organizational responsibilities that are to do with the health and safety of the diggers and of the security of the site.

Above Excavating this well presents a large range of challenges and possible risks.

As a volunteer taking part in an excavation, it is easy to take for granted the work that will have gone into the preparation before the dig begins. Someone will have sent joining instructions and maps to the volunteers, along with equipment lists and information about the excavation and its objectives. On their arrival volunteers will find accommodation or

a campsite, toilets and (if lucky) hot water and a shower. On site there might be a marquee where diggers can take shelter in bad weather, and which they can use for morning, lunch and afternoon tea breaks.

Several lockable huts, similar to those used on building sites, will have been rented and delivered to the site for use as site offices and stores. They will be used to store all the paperwork and recording materials used on site, for meetings, for storing equipment and for processing and storing finds. Valuable equipment and finds need to be taken off site every night, and some electronic equipment such as cameras,

Left and below Reflector jackets are vital to the safety of archaeologists at a dig, particularly on sites where machinery is present.

computers and electronic measuring equipment will need access to an electricity supply because batteries will need to be recharged overnight.

In some countries, these facilities will be set up within a secure compound. Sometimes diggers are accommodated in a school or hostel, while some long-term excavations have their own purpose-built dig houses and offices.

Security and the public

Archaeologists have to walk a delicate line between involving the public in their work and ensuring that the site is not damaged by vandals, metal detectorists or people who walk all

Below Children are often invited to take part in small research excavations, but they should be monitored carefully by an adult at all times.

over the site unaware of the damage they are doing to delicate remains. If the dig is in a remote part of the countryside, this can be less of a problem, but in or on the edge of populated areas and on publicly accessible land it will be necessary to hire and install security fencing, inform the police and perhaps hire a security team to watch the site – otherwise you might return to the site the next day to find that your scientifically precise work has been wrecked by treasure hunters during the night. In some countries, armed guards are a necessity, posted day and night.

Every archaeologist is an evangelist for their cause, and it is natural to want to share information about the site with the public, through the local media and through site tours. However, these are best planned for the last days of the excavation, when most of the work has been completed. It is never a good idea to broadcast to the world that you have found something 'rare, valuable or unusual' unless you want to attract the wrong kind of visitor and sadly, some journalists seem to know of only one kind of headline when it comes to archaeology – one that screams out the monetary value of a find rather than its archaeological value as a piece of information. 'What is it worth?' is a question journalists ask too often about archaeological finds rather than 'what does it mean?'.

Health and safety

Over and above the common-sense issues of site security, there might well be a number of additional reasons why special measures need to be taken to meet the terms of insurance policies and health and safety legislation.

Undertaking a formal risk assessment before working on a site might well seem a long way from the excitement of archaeological research, however it is necessary to make sure that people are safe when they work on site and that adequate measures are in place to ensure that they are not harmed by tools and machinery, by falling sections, by soil heaps that

Above Archaeological work usually carries on even when adverse weather threatens.

Weather and its influence
The local climate can be a decisive factor in the excavation regime. In hot weather conditions, the dig might begin at dawn, involving a very early start to the day, but finishing before noon and the hottest period of the day. After lunch and a siesta, staff might use the afternoons for laboratory work, analysing soil samples or cleaning finds. Excavation does not always stop for rain: gentle rain can produce good working conditions because changes in soil colour are easier to see when the soil is damp and the sunlight is diffused by cloud.

collapse, or by insects, wildlife, dehydration and too much exposure to the sun – to name just a few of the many potential hazards.

As part of the risk assessment, decisions have to be made about where machinery will operate, with clear working zones that nobody else is allowed to enter and a site supervisor to prevent anyone entering that area while machinery, such as dumper trucks and tractors, are operating.

Above This 900-year-old Persian tombstone was stolen from a mosque in Tehran, Iran, and later recovered from a British antiques dealer.

Professional archaeologists usually work on site wearing high-visibility clothing and protective helmets and footwear. Health and safety legislation requires that a first-aid box is available, that a trained first-aider knows how to use it and that everyone on site knows what to do if there is an accident.

Removing the Topsoil

Before the serious archaeology begins, the site has to be prepared by removing the disturbed topsoil and cleaning the site to reveal the undisturbed archaeological features below. Cleaning will help the diggers to get a feel for the site and to answer key questions about where to dig.

Undisturbed archaeology is sometimes found right on the surface of the site, especially in the case of sites that have remained untouched by subsequent agriculture, in which case there is no need to strip turf and topsoil from the site. However, there is often a layer of turf or scrubby vegetation that needs to be removed, and there might also be a layer of plough spoil that has been turned and mixed so many times over the centuries that any material

it contains is of little value to the archaeologist. Test pitting (*see* Excavation Strategies) will help to establish whether or not this is the case.

Stripping the topsoil

On a small excavation, turf and topsoil removal is all done by hand, using a spade, pickaxe and shovel. On larger excavations, the overburden is stripped off by a machine – a task that is often done before the diggers arrive on site.

Above Removal of turf prior to an excavation on the Scottish island of Dun Eistean.

There is a great skill to stripping a site so that archaeological features are cleanly revealed but not damaged. The archaeologist who supervises the stripping of the site needs to have a good understanding of the local soils and geology to be able to tell the difference between disturbed plough soil, 'natural' features and those that are archeologically significant. This is easy enough on a flat site with an even depth of plough soil, or a site on chalk where black soil-filled archaeological features are highlighted against the white of the underlying geology, but it is far less easy when dealing with sticky clay on a hillside. In such circumstances, the rule is to err on the side of caution, grading the site little by little and checking the newly revealed surface at each scrape of the tractor bucket to see whether the soil changes colour or character or whether there are any finds in the soil.

It is better to take off too little over the site overburden than too much – you cannot reconstruct features that are scraped up in a metal tractor bucket. More and more archaeologists enlist the help of metal detectorists at this stage in the opening up of a site, to search the topsoil for metal objects that might be hidden in the soil. These can

Left Hoes are used to penetrate to the next level of a site in the Sudanese desert. Topsoiling becomes more complex when dealing with fine sediment and ditches that tend to fill as quickly as they are dug.

range from discarded bits of tractor and modern nails, to lost children's toys, coins, keys, brooches or buttons. Many will have been lost casually – by someone working or walking in the field – but some might also add important information about the nature of the deposits that form the history of the site.

Cleaning

Before any decisions can be made about where to begin digging, the site is cleaned up and planned. While archaeologists are sometimes accused of taking a relaxed attitude to their own personal appearance, they are obsessive about site cleanliness. 'Spoil' – the soil that has been extracted from the site and is regarded as no longer of any informational use – has to be constantly removed because it gets in the way of those careful observations about change in soil colour on which decisions are made.

So having opened up the site, the next stage for the diggers, while the supervisors and directors ponder the excavation strategy, is to clean all the loose soil and make a drawn and photographic record of the site. Cleaning is best done in dry conditions, because wet soils will smear and obscure the edges of features. Cleaning tools include a trowel and a hoe and – like any house-proud home owner – an old-fashioned brush and dustpan. Archaeologists soon learn particular techniques for cleaning the loose soil away from features. They use the brush to flick it from the surface into the hand shovel or dustpan rather than dragging soil and stone across the feature, which can cause damage.

Spoil tips

The spoil tip (heap), is where all the waste material excavated from the site is placed. To restore the site after the excavation, different parts of the site might have their own separate spoil tips. The first is used to store the turf (if any), which will eventually be put back when the site is refilled. The second might be used to store topsoil – that is the humus-rich soil into which farmers plant their crops, as distinct from the less fertile subsoil that lies underneath, which might make a third tip. All three tips are located well away from areas that might need excavating, but not so far away as to create a long trek for the diggers who empty their buckets and barrows at regular intervals.

Some archaeologists regard creating a good spoil tip as an art, and they design them with all the care of a landscape architect. Grading the spoil tip is critical, so that there is no risk of a landslip. Ergonomic solutions to lifting and transporting soil from the site are considered to avoid back and joint injuries or the risk of diggers slipping off planks – that is why experienced diggers often create spoil tips that resemble archaeological features such as barrows and ziggurats (the terraced temples of ancient Mesopotamia, with ramps that run at a gentle gradient up the sides to the summit).

Above If the ground is particularly solid, you may need to hack to the next level with a pickaxe. This should be used with care.

Above Small finds may be 'missed' and end up submerged in spoil. It is wise to check the spoil heap regularly with a metal detector.

Above (top) Systematic topsoiling requires the turf to be removed in neat slices. These are then replaced when the site is backfilled at the end of the excavation.

Above (bottom) Site features begin to emerge once the top level of soil is removed.

Datum Points and Site Grids

In order to create an overall plan of the site, a 'datum point' is set up that will be used as the reference point for all the other measurements. These measurements are taken to pinpoint the precise location of every feature of an excavation, and to note the exact positions of the key finds.

Above An archaeologist measures the height of a wall from the fixed datum point.

While the initial cleaning of the site is in progress, other archaeologists will be busy selecting the particular point on the site that will be used as the datum point – that is, a fixed location from which all the other measurements on the site are made.

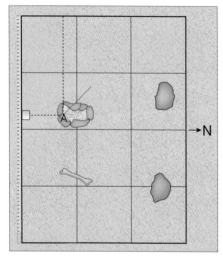

Locating a datum point

Using conventions established by 18th-century surveyors working for the Ordnance Survey, it is established practice to locate the datum point on the south-western edge of the site. Measurements will be taken from that point in an easterly direction first, then in a northerly direction.

The datum point is normally located in a place that gives an uninterrupted view of the whole site, because tape measures will be run from it, and various optical measuring instruments

Left and below Once the datum points are set up at the corners of the site, a tape can be run around the edges, from one corner to the next. The position of features can be plotted by running another tape at right angles to this. In this example, point A is 0.75m (2¹/₂ ft) from the western edge of the site, and 1.75m (5¹/₄ ft) from the southern edge.

rely on it to provide their measurements. If the site is steep, terraced or hilly, several datum points are set up, each overlooking an area of the site. The datum points are sited somewhere that is not likely to be excavated for the duration of dig (which might be several years) or in the future. It is a fixed point that should survive for decades afterward, in the case of research digs, so that archaeologists can revisit the site in the future and locate its features precisely. If no obvious landscape features suggest themselves, such as a building, gate post or fence line, archaeologists will sometimes create their own datum point by hammering a long metal or concrete post into the

Below On this large industrial site, mini-datum points marked with red flags have been set up to help plot the features in the south-western area of the excavation.

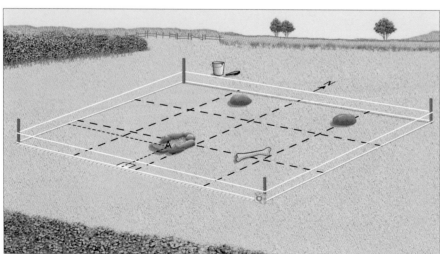

ground, a strategy often deployed if the team expects to revisit the site over a number of years and can be sure that the field won't be cultivated.

Although Global Positioning Systems (GPS; *see* The Importance of Location) now allow archaeologists to pinpoint where on the planet the datum point is, these systems don't make datum points entirely redundant. There are extremely accurate GPS systems that can guide unmanned tractors across a field, ploughing, sowing or harvesting crops without human intervention, however, most systems can pinpoint a location to only within 300mm (12in) – and that is a margin that is large enough to lead to some serious errors on an archaeological site.

Total stations, or EDMs

Achieving pinpoint accuracy and recording in three dimensions once required surveying skills and mathematical dexterity acquired through long practice, using tape measures, a theodolite, measuring staffs and ranging rods – equipment that had not changed much since Greek and Roman road builders or medieval church builders developed their crafts. Fortunately, anyone can now do the same job using a battery-operated device called a total station, also known as electronic distance measuring equipment (EDM; *see* The Importance of Location). The only limitation is that these devices tend to work best in open terrain.

The EDM is placed on the datum point, and its position is fixed using co-ordinates from the GPS (or it might have its own inbuilt GPS). The reflector is taken to the spot on the site where the position needs to be fixed. The EDM bounces a beam of infrared light off the reflector, and the total station's software is then able to produce a set of three dimensional coordinates: it calculates latitude and longitude by combining data from the angle of the beam in relation to the north point and the time it takes for the light to go out and come back, and it calculates heights by taking a reading from the reflector scale.

Site grids

If an EDM is not available, the alternative is to set up a site grid, which will use the datum point as the starting point (*see illustration opposite*). Typically, the grid is marked out using tape measures and by hammering iron pegs into the ground to mark out the grid squares, usually at 5m (16ft) intervals. The pegs themselves are used throughout the excavation as mini datum points, from which measurements can be taken within that 5m/16ft grid square.

Above An EDM being used to plot the height of a feature above or below the site datum.

This grid might be used to produce an initial plan of the site by plotting the edges of all the features, using a six-figure grid system. If the co-ordinates of the datum point are 100/100, the grid is used to measure how many metres to the east, then to the north of the datum point the feature lies. If the written grid reference for a pit is 270/065, the pit is 27m (88ft) east of the datum point and 6.5m (21ft) north.

Above A datum point is being set up on Mount Erebus, Antarctica.

National grids

Some countries have a national grid system that archaeologists can use as the basis for pinpointing the location of their site datum. Datum base points, from which all heights above and below sea level are measured, are located around the world – at Newlyn in Cornwall, for example, at Cardona Island Lighthouse in Puerto Rico, and at Kortright in Sierra Leone. In countries with no national grid, archaeologists depend on local grids established at some past date for military or engineering use, or on GPS.

The Initial Site Plan

Once the grid is in place, it then becomes possible to create an accurate plan of the site, which will show the features that have been revealed through cleaning. A detailed plan of the site is important before the dig begins, because it will be a record of the original conditions of the site.

Field archaeology consists of a series of repetitive processes, one of which is maintaining a drawn and photographic record of the site while it is being excavated – in effect, making as accurate a copy as possible on paper and on camera of the site that is about to be destroyed. This may sound brutal, but it is the truth – as soon as undisturbed archaeological material is removed from a site, it is impossible to put it back in the same way that it was found. As most people cannot rely on having an accurate memory, drawing and photography are the tools that archaeologists have developed as

the means by which a site can be 'reconstructed' at a later stage – albeit in the virtual reality of a computer model rather than physically.

Drawing equipment

Although archaeologists like the drawings to look clean, clear and pleasing, this is essentially a technical activity rather than an aesthetic one. Archaeologists do not sit by the side of the trench and seek to create a three-dimensional sketch of the site using shading and perspective. Instead, the plan is strictly two dimensional, and it is achieved by using a combination of

Above Archaeologists continually refer to their plans of the site throughout the excavation.

the site grid and a sheet of graph paper as a guide. Graph paper is covered in a grid of lines, and these will correspond to the lines of the site grid that has already been laid out using pegs hammered into the ground.

To start making a plan, a drawing board – a light but firm rectangle of wood – is necessary. A drawing board is typically 750mm (30in) in length and 500mm (20in) or so in width, so it is small enough to be carried around and to work with on site, but large enough

Above The drawn record begins as soon as features begin to appear. Working as a pair, one archaeologist measures the position and dimensions of a visible feature within the squares of the drawing grid, while the other records this on a scaled drawing.

Left A simple scale can be applied to the drawing by correlating the squares of the graph paper to the drawing grid.

The result is a two-dimensional plan of the outline of the features visible at this stage, which will be the top of the features, before excavation begins. Further information is added to the plan once it has been drawn. Reference numbers are allocated to each feature, and these numbers are then written by the corresponding feature on the plan, along with the height of the top of the feature above sea level, which is measured using a theodolite and site datum or EDM.

Site photography

Finally, everything that has been drawn is also photographed as a further record of the site. In preparation for photography, the site may be given a final cleaning, which will include the removal of all tools and people from the site so that they do not appear in the photograph. However, what must appear in the photographs is a scale, usually consisting of a pair of surveyor's ranging rods, which are 2m- (6½ft-) long poles, divided into four 500mm (20in) segments, alternately painted red and white. One of these is laid on the site to line up with the vertical axis of the photograph, and another is laid parallel to the horizontal axis. These will give an approximate sense of the size of the site and features in the resulting photograph.

Below Each feature on the site is photographed as well as drawn.

to accommodate a sheet of metric graph paper, which measures about 594mm (23in) x 420mm (28in).

The graph paper is secured to the drawing board using a masking tape or adhesive tape that will be easy to remove at a later stage without tearing the paper. A sheet of heavy-grade weatherproof tracing paper is laid over the graph paper, secured to the drawing board with the same type of tape. For drawing, an HB pencil and a good non-smudging eraser is suitable.

Tapes and grids

For taking measurements, both a long 20m (65ft) tape measure and a short 3m (10ft) one will be necessary, as well as a drawing grid, an invaluable aid. The drawing grid consists of a frame, measuring 1m (3ft) x 1m (3ft), with wires or strings subdividing the frame into 100mm (40in) squares.

The grid is laid on the ground on top of the features that you want to draw; the grid squares correspond to the squares on the graph paper on your drawing board, and planning the site is a question of transferring the outlines of the features that you can see on the ground on to the tracing paper, using the underlying graph paper as a guide.

Making the plan

The drawing grid is used for drawing smaller details, but first it is best to draw the outlines of the major features using the site grid. This is achieved by running the long tape measure between two pegs on opposite sides of the site and marking on your tracing paper the precise points at which the tape intersects the edges of the feature. The only way to achieve the required degree of accuracy is to stand directly over the point, looking vertically down on to the tape measure – standing to take measurements at an oblique angle will result in a reading that could be out by 100mm/4in or more.

Having marked on the tracing paper the point where the tape and feature coincide, you can then use the shorter tape measure to take further spot measurements from the tape at intervals of 100mm (4in), 200mm (8in), 300mm (12in), 400mm (16in) or 500mm (20in). How many measurements you take will depend on the shape and complexity of the feature. Straight-sided ditches, for example, will need fewer spot measurements than a serpentine one. The shape of the feature is then sketched in using the measured points as a guide.

Typical Site Features

Once a site is cleaned up, what is found should not come as too much of a surprise to the archaeologists if the preparation work was done in advance. In addition, some common features are often encountered on a typical archaeological site, and these can provide clues to the site before digging.

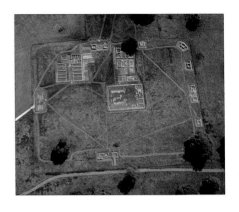

Opening up the site involves removing soil that has been disturbed by natural, human or animal activity, such as tree-root disturbance, ploughing or burrowing, to expose features that have not been disturbed. What survives will depend on the age of the deposits, and on climate and soil conditions. For example, in waterlogged dry or cold conditions (*see* Vulnerable Finds), more organic material survives, such as clothing, basketry, paper and flesh, whereas in acidic conditions bones might not survive but wood does. This is why few human remains are associated with Hadrian's Wall; the moorland soil destroys bone, but there

are well-preserved written records, consisting of tablets of wood. Knowing the soil and weather conditions will provide information to archaeologists.

Colours in the soil

On a typical site, surviving structures are mostly the remains of buildings and property boundaries, pits and hearths, tracks and roadways, and industrial remains, such as kilns or debris. There are also burial sites, as well as sites interpreted as 'ritual', often because their purpose is not understood.

In most cases, these are visible in the ground as circles, rectangles or lines of soil that are different in colour from

Above This site is recognizable as a Roman fort from the 'playing card' shape of the outer walls and the barrack blocks within.

the 'natural', or background, soil. These colour differences are often the result of the slow rotting of organic remains, such as timber posts or beams that once stood in the ground.

The importance of simple soil stains and subtle colour differences is spectacularly demonstrated at Sutton Hoo, in Suffolk, England. This site is renowned for its two Anglo-Saxon cemeteries of the 6th and early 7th centuries. One of these cemeteries, when excavated in the 1930s, was

Above This area of raised ground at Great Burwood Estate, Essex, England, puzzled archaeologists, who sunk two trial trenches into the earth following an initial survey. They found the remains of a prominent 17th-century dwelling, which they were able to date partly from the trading goods found at the site.

Left The excavation of the burial ship at Sutton Hoo, East Anglia, UK, in 1939.

Right Kalut-e Gird, a circular fortress close to the Afghan border, was buried beneath creeping sand dunes for many years.

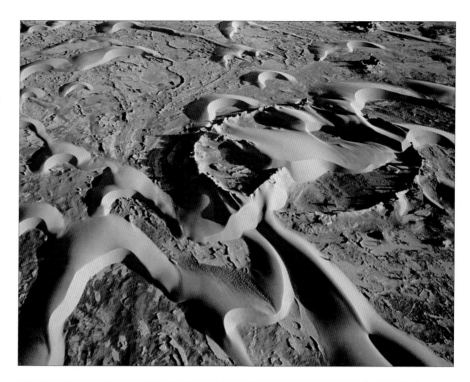

found to contain an undisturbed ship burial and a wealth of brooches, shoulder claps and royal regalia of gold inlaid with red garnet, all of which can now be seen in the British Museum. Photographs of the 27m- (88½ft-) long ship at the heart of the cemetery show what appears to be a complete hull with all its planks in place. In fact, the timber had disappeared, and everything known about the boat results from the painstaking care with which the excavators traced barely discernible stains from the rotted wood that survived in the sand in which the boat was laid upon.

Explaining the differences

After a site has been abandoned by its original users, ditches and pits slowly accumulate silt, leaves, grass and weeds as they fill through the natural processes of wind, rain and soil erosion. Ditches might, for example, provide a habitat for wetland plants that rot to a darker colour than the surrounding grassland; finer silts are washed into the hollow by rain or the slow collapse of the sides.

Experimental archaeology has been conducted that involved excavating pits and monitoring the speed in which they fill and what they fill with. It has been established that the process is fast to begin with, but slows down over time, so that distinctive hollows marking the position of a pit or a ditch might be visible for many decades after the abandonment of the site. The implication of this work is that our ancestors had to keep their ditches and gullies well-maintained if they were to be effective in draining water, or to keep out animals. Seasonal recutting of ditches must have been the norm.

What do they mean?

Looked at in plan, without any further excavation, the shape of the features will often tell archaeologists a great deal about the nature and age of the site.

Above Post holes are evidence of former boundaries on this Bronze Age track.

The archaeology of a post hole

Post holes are a common find in archaeology. They represent the remains of timber posts set into the ground, usually as part of a fence or wall. Some posts have sharp, pencil-shaped ends and are hammered straight into the ground. Bigger, flat-bottomed posts are usually set into a specially dug hole or pit; the space between the post and the edges of the hole is then backfilled with soil and small rocks, which are rammed hard to ensure that the post stays upright. When archaeologists excavate post holes they typically find the packing material, represented by soil of a different colour to the post itself. The post will either show up as an area of dark organic soil, if the post rotted within the hole, or as a ghost of the post, if the post was deliberately pulled out of the post hole to be reused elsewhere as part of the dismantling of the structure. In the latter case, the soil filling the space once occupied by the post will be derived from the slow process of the natural erosion and worm action, gradually filling the hole.

Archaeologists have dug enough sites to recognize common types: circular ditches, depending on their diameter, might be evidence of a burial mound, or of a hut. Long lines of small stake holes might represent a fence or palisade. Larger post holes could be a house, hut, byre or workshop, if set in a rectangular pattern, perhaps with smaller stake holes representing internal divisions.

Some or all of these could represent human activity from any time between the Mesolithic and the later medieval period, but clues such as the size of the features and the overall assemblage – the mix of features that are found in association with each other – enable a seasoned archaeologist to make a good guess at what the site contains just from looking at the overall pattern of feature, even before excavation.

Contexts and Site Codes

Archaeologists use certain terms to describe the features found during an excavation. It is important that a digger understands this terminology to make sure records are kept accurately. Because the terminology can be confusing, sometimes reference numbers are used.

Some archaeologists object to the use of descriptive terms such as 'ditch', 'feature', 'fill', 'deposit', 'layer' or 'soil'. They try to be as objective and as scientific as possible and use neutral terms to describe the material they excavate. Avoiding evaluative terms is not a question of slavish adherence to an archaeological orthodoxy; it is often the case that the interpretation of a site or a feature changes as you excavate it. Rather than rewriting the site notes each time a feature that was initially described as a pit turns into a grave, it is better to use neutral terminology during the data-gathering stage and reserve judgement about the function or meaning of the context until all the evidence is available, as part of the analytical post-excavation phase.

Use of the term 'context'

The neutral term increasingly used to describe the material that archaeologists excavate is 'context', and every context is given a unique

Above The first trench sunk at a dig may reveal numerous 'contexts'.

identification number, or 'site code', as it is excavated. The word is a good one because the deposits or layers that we excavate are quite literally the contexts, or containers, for the finds that lie within them.

However, the term context is also used for a phase in the site's history that might not have any physical counterpart. For example, in between the digging of a ditch, which leaves a physical cut in the surrounding soil and rock, and the filling of the ditch, which is represented by stones and soil that wash into the ditch from the top and sides, there is a period when the ditch is open. This open phase might last for many years, but if the ditch is kept clean and periodically recut, that passage of time is not represented by a physical imprint. However, the passage of time is recognized by archaeologists by allocating a context number to the open ditch. Technically, anything that represents a unique event in the sequence of events that makes up the history of the site is a context – because a period of time passes between the digging of the ditch and the next stage in its history, the open ditch has its own context number.

Other archaeologists use a variety of terms to distinguish different types of context. Some use the word 'locus' to describe a soil deposit, and some

Left The layers of soil excavated from a section of the site each represent an individual 'context', reflecting the passage of time.

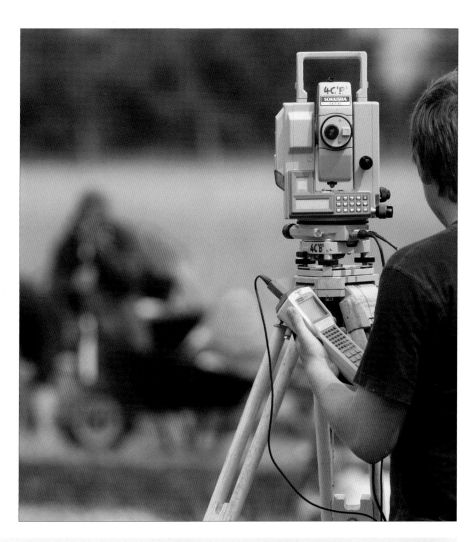

Right Using EDM, site surveyors can pinpoint the location of a demarcated feature, or a 'section' marked out to excavate that feature, before the dig gets fully underway. This supplies a basic 'context' for any finds unearthed in that spot.

avoid the issue simply by referring to every context by its reference number, which might be prefixed with a letter indicating whether it is soil, a wall or a floor. Perhaps the most common practice is a combination of the two: using context numbers as a scientifically neutral record of the site, but using more easily understood descriptive words as an aid to communicating with fellow diggers and for interpreting the site as it is excavated. Hence, the supervisor might refer to 'that deposit' to describe a 'layer' of 'soil' forming part of the 'fill' of a 'cut', such as a 'ditch'. You might also hear the word 'feature' used to describe a post hole or solid structures, such as walls, floors, cobbled yards or roads. With these philosophical and terminological thoughts to ponder, our first time archaeologist finally gets the go-ahead to begin to dig.

Who does what on site?

Within the digging hierarchy, some or all of the tasks involved in excavating and documenting the site might be entrusted to a specialist, to ensure an accurate record is made.

For example, a site photographer will only be involved in taking pictures, while an illustrator or draughtsperson will be primarily responsible for all the site plans and section drawings. There might also be a surveyor, whose job is to compile and maintain a log of all the grid measurements taken on site. There will almost certainly be a finds specialist, whose job is to ensure that all finds are labelled, conserved and securely stored – though volunteers from among the diggers are often recruited for a day or so in the finds shed to help with this work and learn how finds are treated on site. If the excavation requires it, there might be an environmentalist with the equipment and skills to take and analyse soil samples on site.

On smaller digs, some or all of these tasks might be the responsibility of the site supervisor or the director. Supervisors will often be keen to train individual diggers to do their own recording, on the grounds that the person who knows the material best is the person who has the intimate understanding of the feature that comes from having excavated it.

Above A supervisor is always there to monitor the diggers. Typically, one is assigned to manage each of the main areas of the site, such as individual trenches.

Preparing to Dig a Section

A 'section' dig will allow archaeologists to have an interior look at a site before the real excavation begins. Archaeologists use certain terms to describe the features that might be found in this and other digs, and it is important that a digger understands them to make sure records are kept accurately.

Above A feature being excavated in two sections, each of which will have its own code.

The site as a whole has been cleaned up, gridded and planned, and the initial excavation strategy discussed. Sometimes the excavators will decide to put sections through some of the features in order to investigate their stratigraphy and contents.

A section is a vertical incision cut through an archaeological feature, such as a ditch or a pit. Like a slice through a layer cake, it reveals the different colours and textures of soil that fill the feature, and the sequence and contents help archaeologists to date and understand past human activity on the site.

Preparing a section

A first-time digger may be asked to dig a section of a small ditch. The first task will be to do a mini site preparation exactly like the one that has already been done for the site as a whole, including cleaning it up once again. Archaeologists are obsessive about keeping their working areas clean, treating a site as if it were a scientific laboratory for the systematic gathering of data, and ensuring that the subtle differences in soil colour that mark the edges of features are not obscured by loose or trampled soil.

The next step will be to demarcate a length of ditch to excavate. An area that will be comfortable to work in will need to be marked out, but it shouldn't be so large that it will involve extra work without gaining additional information – a 2m (6½ft) stretch of ditch will usually suffice. Both ends of the area to be excavated should be marked using nails and string. These represent the points at which the sections will later be drawn. They need to be at precise right angles to the line of the ditch and parallel to each other, otherwise the section that is revealed will be distorted and will not represent the relationships between the different deposits filling the ditch.

Photographs and codes

Before excavation, photographs are taken of the ditch. A scale is included in the picture, consisting of a pole or rod typically 50cm (20in) or 1m (3¼ft) in length, divided like a ruler into 100mm intervals by red and white coloured bands. Without the scale, it will be difficult for anyone to judge how big the ditch is from a photograph: with it, the width and depth can be estimated.

Every photograph taken is logged in a register, and a unique code for the area of the site will be issued. This code will be used to identify everything that

Left With the topsoil removed, and features revealed by the changing colours in the soil, decisions can be made about where to dig a section in order to take a closer look.

Above An opened trench, like every feature on the site, will also have its own unique code. For example, if the trench is the ninth area to be opened on the site, it might be called Trench 9. That unique number is also recorded on the master plan of the site and entered into a 'context register', along with the location of the trench.

results from the excavation of the ditch — not just the photographs, but also the various recording sheets (these will be explained later), plans, section drawings, grid coordinates, finds and soil samples.

The site itself will have its own unique code. In the UK this usually consists of three letters derived from the name of the site and then two numbers, denoting the year in which the work commenced. So the whole of the dig might be known as AHF07, meaning Abbey Home Farm 2007.

Digging a section

In order to reveal the section, it is necessary to remove the soil that is filling the feature. However, that soil itself is a vital part of the evidence for the history of the site, so the soil has to be removed systematically, layer by layer. As the soil is loosened with a trowel it is vital to collect all the visible finds from the layer. On some sites, the loose soil is also sieved (sifted) to look for finds trapped in unbroken clumps or too small to be seen by the excavator, including microscopic environmental finds such as seeds, pollens, insects and snails, charcoal and fish bones.

Above (top) The multiple features visible in this Roman burial site are individual graves.

Above (bottom) Excavators work in pairs to uncover the remains of an ancient road.

Knowing exactly where to place a section takes great skill, but there is no foolproof method of ensuring that the section you decide to cut will recover all the data. For example, when excavating a section of ditch, you might find that the ditch itself contains several additional features: perhaps a post hole from a gate post, or perhaps a layer of burnt stones and charcoal. Unless by sheer luck the vertical section happens to coincide with these features, the section alone will miss them and thus not be a complete record of the ditch. For that reason, every feature that is

found within another feature is also planned and sectioned, and a record is made of the vertical and horizontal extent of every layer that the excavator encounters, to ensure a full record.

The excavator's aim, therefore, is to record all the features in three dimensions: vertical section records show how deep each layer is and how each one relates to adjacent layers; plan records show how far each layer extends in a horizontal direction. Sections and plans form two of the most important records that result from modern scientific archaeology.

Excavating a Ditch

After all the preparation work, which may have involved section digging, the aim for the team is to begin excavating the first context in its entirety. This involves the very difficult task of judging where the existing layer stops and where a new one begins.

The go-ahead has finally been given to make a start on excavating the first ditch. The first deposit is removed, using a trowel to remove the surface of the fill. Beginning at one end of the ditch, a mini trench is cut into the soil, loosening the earth with a scraping action, with the pointed heel of the trowel pulled toward the digger. Proceeding with care until the digger knows what the fill is like, small amounts of soil are removed, with the loose trowelled soil regularly swept up with a hand shovel and put into a container, such as a plastic bucket.

Depending on the nature of the material being excavated, the bucket might simply be emptied into a wheelbarrow – and when that is full, it might be wheeled away and the material dumped on the spoil tip. However, if the site is likely to yield small finds, the material might be sieved before it is discarded. The sieving (sifting) process involves breaking down the soil and passing it through a series of sieves (screens) of finer and finer mesh size. Some soils simply will not break down into finer particles when wet, and become as hard as concrete when dry. Such soils might be wet sieved using a hose, after they have first been soaked by standing them in a bucket of water.

As the digger gets to know the soil being worked, the speed of excavation will pick up. Heavier tools, such as a mattock or hoe, might be used if the layer is empty of finds and of monotonous consistency – which is the norm for many ditch fills. The way the

Above When systematic line trowelling is in action, it is important that the excavated part of the trench is not walked across.

dig proceeds reflects the expectations of what the dig fill is like. Even so, the digger should be constantly alert for finds, or for any change in soil colour and consistency that marks a transition from one layer to another, or perhaps a separate feature within a ditch.

Looking for interfaces

The places where a digger is most likely to encounter the first signs of a change are at the edges of the ditch, because this is where the deposit is often the shallowest. When a ditch begins to fill up after it has fallen out of use, soil from the sides falls to the bottom first and tends to form deeper layers in the middle of the ditch, trailing to shallower layers at the sides.

The blunt reality of archaeology, however, is that diggers very often dig through the next layer without recognizing the change. The division between one layer and the next is called the horizon, and sometimes this can be quite sharp, especially when dealing with pits that are filled manually over a period of time, with clear changes from a brown to a black layer, or from silt to fine gravel. Just as

Left Ditches are one of the commonest types of feature found on archaeological sites: this one at Pattnam in Kerala, southern India, marks a boundary in the historic trading port of Muziris and it yielded pottery evidence of ancient trade between India and Rome dating back some 3,000 years.

often, however, this interface is gradual rather than abrupt, especially if the soil has been well and truly mixed up by centuries of worm and root activity.

Excavating in spits

To minimize the risk of going too deep and penetrating a separate layer within the ditch fill, a digger usually takes the soil down in 'spits', by first removing a depth of 30mm (1in) to 50mm (2in) at one end of the trench. If no change in the soil is detected in that small area of the trench, the same depth of soil is taken out again across the whole of the trench. Then the whole process begins again – taking down another 30mm (1in) to 50mm (2in) in a small area of the trench before excavating a bigger area.

The digger will keep checking the sections that mark the two ends of the trench, and the vertical slice through the ditch that gets deeper as digging continues downward. This provides additional vital clues to the character of the soil being taken out, and will show clearly whether the digger has gone too far and dug into a new layer.

A nervous first-time digger shouldn't worry over the risks of doing the job wrong: the site supervisor's job is to keep checking the work and to help the digger interpret what is being found. With their knowledge and experience they will also help the digger distinguish between the fill of the ditch and the 'natural' surface, which is to say the virgin soil or gravel or rock into which the ditch was cut. It is this natural surface that will form the sides and bottom of the emptied-out ditch, once it is fully excavated.

Once emptied, the ditch will then be revealed again in the shape and form that it was when it began to fill up: excavating the ditch will help to reveal past, long-buried landscape features. How long that ditch was a feature of the landscape, why it was dug, how it was filled and how it relates to other site features are questions that the digger ultimately hopes to help answer.

Right Spit excavation is in progress amid the cramped surroundings of an inner-city site.

The basics of line trowelling

1 The purpose of line trowelling is to clean the site and reveal colour changes in the soil.

2 Using the edge of the trowel, soil is loosened and drawn back toward the diggers.

3 Colour changes may indicate buried archaeology, so loose soil is routinely cleared from the trowelled area.

4 This resulting 'spoil' is collected in a bucket for dry sieving (sifting) for any small finds the digger did not spot.

Describing Deposits

The physical appearance of the deposit needs to be recorded accurately and in detail as it is excavated, with additional observations or amendments being added as the digging proceeds. Paperwork rules an excavation just as much as any other sphere of life.

Before digging for very long, the site supervisor will arrive with a context recording sheet and sit down with the digger to explain the procedure for recording the excavation. The examples given here are taken from the practice commonly used by British archaeologists, but similar recording systems are widely used all over the world, perhaps with slightly different terminology.

Increasingly, as electronic equipment becomes less expensive, more reliable and easy to use, laptops or hand-held computers are used to record information about a context. However, even where data is captured digitally in the field, a paper record is also kept, on the belt and braces principle that if a computer disc is lost, stolen or destroyed, there is always another back-up record.

Allocating context numbers

As a digger excavates a trench or ditch, every deposit or feature encountered will be given its own unique context number. This number is obtained from the context register, and is allocated in numerical sequence – so the upper-most layer of, for example, Trench 9 will be given the context number 900 (the next layer will be 901, the next 902 and so on). The context number is written at the head of the recording sheet, along with the name of the trench and its grid references.

Right Regularly spraying the sides of an open trench with water will help to bring out the different colours of the soil layers.

The rest of the sheet is used to record any observations about the physical appearance of the deposit. But rather than leave the description of the deposit to the subjective judgement of the digger, the sheet has a number of tick boxes that serve as prompts for recording the main characteristics.

Soil colour

As it dries, soil changes colour, so the deposit is ideally described when it is damp: sprucing it up with a light spray is permitted – in fact, diggers working on sunny dry conditions keep a sprayer handy for this purpose, delivering a fine mist of water to the surface of the soil sufficient to restore its colour, but not to wash the particles away.

Above Accurate description is key to the recording of archaeological features.

First, the digger will describe the basic colour of the deposit: black, brown, white, yellow, orange, and so on. However, soils are rarely all of one simple colour, so archaeologists tend to describe the predominant hue, using such terms as blackish, whitish, yellowish, orangey. The description might also note if the soil is consistently of that colour, or whether it grades from light to dark, or vice versa. As the digger excavates the site, he or she will also be asked to note how easy it is to distinguish the layer from adjoining layers – whether the 'horizon clarity' is good, medium or poor.

Above Rolling the earth between fingers will help to assess soil compaction.

Above The shape and content of a feature are recorded on a context recording sheet.

Soil composition

Composition relates to the size of the particles that make up the deposit, ranging from the finest – clay and silt – to middling – sand (particles up to 2mm (⅒in) in size) and gravel (2–4mm (⅒–3⁄₂₀in)) – to the largest – pebbles (4–60mm (3⁄₂₀–2⅓in)), cobbles (60–250mm (2⅓–10in)) and boulders (more than 250mm (10in)). Once again, it is not common for soils to have a consistent composition, and archaeologists often end up using descriptions that combine two or more terms, such as silty sand (a sandy deposit with some silt) or sandy silt

(vice versa). With larger material, such as gravels, pebbles, cobbles and boulders, it is useful to note the particle size range and the roundedness – whether sharp and angular, rounded and smooth or in between.

Soil compaction

Compaction describes the strength of the deposit when placed under pressure. For fine-grained deposits such as clay, silt or sand, the test is to try to mould a moist sample with your fingers. If it crumbles it is friable, and if its is easily moulded, mouldable with strong pressure or resistant to

moulding it is described as soft, firm and hard, respectively. Coarser-grained deposits, such as gravels, pebbles and so on are described as loose if they are not self-supporting, friable if they crumble easily, firm if they keep their form under pressure and compact if they are impossible to break.

Variations can occur even within one layer – for example, a road surface or a cobbled yard might have different patterns of composition and compaction, reflecting wear and tear from the use and erosion of the surface. This fact will be brought out in the plans and photographs of the feature, but it also needs to be described on the context recording sheet.

Inclusions

The term 'inclusions' describes any other material in the layer, and this can include natural materials, such as snail shells, or materials resulting from human activity, such as charcoal, bone fragments, shell, worked flint, 'alien' stone that is different from the natural geology, pottery, daub, baked clay, tile, brick and so on. These are described in terms of their frequency (rare 1–3 per cent, sparse 3–7 per cent, moderate 10–20 per cent, common 20–30 per cent, very common 30–40 per cent and abundant 40–50 per cent), and in terms of their size (smears, flecks, and small, medium or large inclusions).

A typical recording sheet

Every organization has its own design when it comes to context recording sheets, but they all record the same core information about the context:
• The character of the deposit e.g. colour and article size.
• The context number and its relationship to other contexts.
• An interpretation and discussion saying how you think the context was formed.
• Reference numbers of any soil samples, photographs, drawings and finds, such as, pot, bone, wood or leather.

Right A context recording sheet from the Museum of London Archaeology Service.

Above Students at an archaeology open day practice recording a scatter of 'inclusions' such as worked flints, using a drawing grid.

Finds in Context

As a layer is carefully excavated, the digger will try to recover all the artefacts it contains, layer by layer, and the finds from each context will be recorded and stored separately. The individual finds have the potential to help archaeologists understand more about the history of the site.

After a couple of hours excavating the first layer of a ditch, the work for a digger can become a little bit routine and monotonous. This is when a digger may become a little careless and, for example, might inadvertently clip the edge of a piece of pottery with a trowel, causing it to flake, with spots of orange flecks appearing in the soil. A digger should always trowel with care – it is difficult to know when you might come across a find.

Finds trays

The supervisor might send the digger to see the finds supervisor, who will explain what happens to the material found during the excavation. First the digger will be given a plastic container, such as a tray or a bucket, and a waterproof label, on which the site code and context number is written in waterproof ink. The tray is where the digger will store all the finds that come from that context; as soon as another

Above This pot 'chimney' uncovered on a site at Heywoods, Barbados, will be painstakingly taken apart, and the relationship between each piece carefully recorded.

deposit is encountered, a new number and tray will be supplied to keep the finds from each layer separate.

Depending on the nature of the site, finds such as pottery, brick, tile, bone or iron slag are regarded as routine – the context recording sheet enables the

Below The recovered bones in the tray were found during an excavation at a medieval burial site. The markers in the earth indicate the position of individual graves.

Right Special bagged finds are tagged into the earth at the exact position in which they were found. The location can then be recorded using a total station or by taking measurements manually.

Dealing with uncommon finds

1 If you find something out of the ordinary, ask your supervisor to take a look. The find may need to be placed in a sealed bag for labelling.

2 Label the bag with the site name, day number and context number before placing it in the tray with the other finds from that context.

Above A 3,500-year-old wooden bridge support is surrounded by layers of tagged stratigraphy.

digger to comment on the quantity and variety of material from the deposit, but no further action is required on the digger's part, other than to deliver the labelled trays to the finds shed at the end of the day. (*For more about the finds shed, see* Processing Finds on Site.)

Special finds

Some finds are regarded as 'special', though the definition of special varies from site to site. On some sites, artefacts are so rare that every single find is recorded in detail. On sites that are rich in material, perhaps only the diagnostically significant finds will be given special treatment: for example, finds that can be dated in absolute terms (coins) or in relative terms (brooches). Alternatively, objects might be given a privileged status if their precise position might be important for the interpretation of the site – for example, objects in a grave, carefully laid out in a significant position around the body of the deceased, or a pit whose contents might have been deposited in a significant order as part of a ritual.

In all cases, special finds (which are sometimes referred to as 'small finds') are treated to a higher level of recording and description. As well as being given a unique number, the precise find spot will be recorded in three dimensions, using EDM equipment or

a theodolite and tape measures (*see* The Initial Site Plan), and the details will be entered into a special finds register and noted on the context recording sheet.

As the site is excavated, the digger will learn what is commonplace and what is special, and if something unusual is encountered, the digger will seek guidance before going any further. Special techniques apply to the extraction of fragile materials, metal objects and material that might be subjected to DNA testing or carbon dating.

Describing relationships

Back at the ditch, the digger will find a new layer emerging, which might be of a different colour and consistency to the one that was being trowelled. The entire first layer from the ditch has been removed, so the digger plans, photographs and assigns a number to the new deposit. In recording the new context, the digger has to decide what relationship exists between this deposit and the first. The relationship can be very simple: in this case the second deposit is entirely covered by the first. But there are several other possibilities that a digger might encounter: two deposits can abut each other, and one can entirely surround another (this is called a lenticular deposit). Most importantly of all for phasing, one context can cut through another.

Being honest about what you find

Sometimes the precise relationship of one deposit to another isn't always crystal clear. You might not even be entirely certain that there are two separate layers, because one blends gradually into another or one is similar to the next – just with fewer inclusions. It is here that experience counts for so much: what is puzzling to a first-time digger might be something that a seasoned digger has seen many times before.

For this reason, context recording sheets have an area for discussion of the evidence, which allows the digger to record comments and changing interpretations as he or she works. This can be used to make observations arising from an intimate relationship with that patch of soil. Relevant observations that might affect the interpretation of the evidence and its reliability might be to note the methods and conditions under which the digger worked (for example, rapid work under salvage conditions, heavy rain, poor light), what the weather and soil conditions were like (waterlogged, frozen, baked hard by the sun), or whether there was evidence of tree-root disturbance or animal burrowing.

Reaching 'the Natural'

The aim of excavation is to unravel the history of archaeological features by removing and examining the deposits one at a time, in the reverse order from that in which they were laid down. This process continues until the only material left is the natural geological surface.

Above The layers of an opened context are ready for examination by an archaeologist.

It can take a few days of digging before a digger is nearly finished excavating a ditch (*see* Excavating a Ditch). This will be a process of discovery for someone who is a novice, finding out how to excavate and record the site and what secrets lie hidden in the ground. Sometimes an unexpected surprise might appear at the base of the ditch. For example, a water channel constructed of stone called a 'box culvert'.

Seeking the natural

If there is a surprise at the base of the ditch, such as a box culvert, it won't have reached a fully excavated stage. To do so will involve dismantling the culvert or other structure, but first it has to be given a context number, cleaned, drawn and photographed, and its coordinates plotted – the same repetitive pattern that is part of every context, deposit and feature.

After filling in the context sheet describing the structure, the digger can begin to take it apart. This can be a sad task because it often involves the destruction of something that had been beautifully constructed; in the case of a box culvert, it will have flat stones forming the base and top, and supporting stones running along the length of the ditch to form a rectangular channel, or conduit.

Removing the conduit is necessary to confirm whether or not there are any further deposits beneath the culvert, including any finds that might help to date it. Although the digger is destroying something that has survived for many centuries, that person might be consoled with the thought that plenty more of it survives below the ground. Once there are no further finds and the supervisor is satisfied that the digger has reached what archaeologists call 'the natural' – meaning the natural geological surface that has been unmodified by human activity – the excavation will reach a conclusion.

Recording the cut

Before the digger prepares to clean up, photograph and draw the empty ditch, it is important to remember that empty features also need a context number. The open empty ditch itself represents a stage in the history of the

Left Archaeologists penetrate to the Bronze-Age level of an ancient site in Sinop, Turkey.

The archaeology of a box culvert

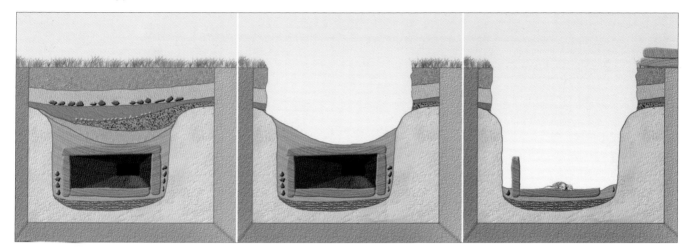

1 This section through a Roman culvert, used to take water from a spring to a water tank, shows the ditch originally dug to lay down the culvert, the culvert itself, made from stone, and the fill above.

2 By this stage, the top levels have been excavated and recorded: the top two layers are cultivated topsoil and a layer of subsoil directly below. Next comes the Roman ditch fill, dated by the pottery fragments in the soil.

3 By the third and final stage, the culvert has been opened to see what lies within: perhaps nothing, perhaps a coin lost by the person who made the culvert, or perhaps the skeleton of a long dead frog or rat!

site. This type of feature is described as a 'cut', naturally enough, because it cuts through another feature – in this case the natural geology.

Various terms are used to record cuts, starting with basic dimensions, such as length, width and depth (with maximum, minimum and average measurements if these vary). The shape can be linear, or it can be square, rectangular, circular, oval, sub-circular or sub-oval or irregular. Linear and irregular features can sometimes also

be described as straight, curving or curvilinear. The orientation of the cut should also be recorded.

If the cut has discernible corners, they are described as straight, rounded or irregular. The sides can be vertical, U-shaped, V-shaped or irregular. The opposing side of the cut might be symmetrical or asymmetrical, and the gradient can be shallow (less than 45 degrees), moderate (45 degrees) or steep (more than 45 degrees). The sides can also be stepped, and the base can be flat, tapered or curved (concave or convex).

The digger's observations

Free text areas of the recording sheet can be used to make interpretative observations: for example, what, at the end of the day, does the digger think of the site? In discussion with the site supervisor, the conclusion might be that the ditch was dug to house the stone culvert, which itself was constructed to carry water from a spring that has yet to be located somewhere higher up the hill. Water was channelled

Left The remains of a Victorian drainage system were uncovered on an industrial site.

from the spring to a group of buildings that are being excavated lower down the hillside site.

The interpretation should include all the evidence that supports the theory about the construction, use and disuse of the feature, based on the information gained from its shape. In this example, the ditch is narrow, with steep regular sides and flat bottom, and there is a shallow gradient, suggesting that it was dug specifically as a channel to house the culvert – it was not dug for another purpose and later used as a culvert. If the ditch had remained open for any period of time, the sides would be more eroded and would have a shallower gradient.

The digger will also try to explain the origin of the deposits in the ditch: whether they are the result of deliberate deposition or from a natural process. The fact that the fill of the ditch is uniform supports the conclusion that the ditch was cut, the culvert laid and the ditch filled again in a short period of time. If the ditch had been left open, there would have been a slow build up of silts and vegetation that would leave distinct bands of soil of different colours and compositions.

Section Drawings and Photographs

Once features are fully excavated, the vertical sections are drawn and photographed to show how the excavated deposits fit together and as a permanent record of what was removed from the site. Section drawings are one of the most informative components of a site's recording.

Above Drawing a section to record the different layers filling the feature.

In many ways the section drawing encapsulates the story of the feature by capturing a slice through its contents. However, in some cases it will provide only a partial story – in the ditch with the box culvert (*see* Reaching the 'Natural'), for example, it only tells about events that happened after the ditch or pit began to fill. This is often the point at which it ceased to be used for its original purpose – although this final stage can have its own interesting story, because sometimes pits or ditches are deliberately closed by filling them with ritual deposits. All this information is captured in the drawing of the section.

Preparing for a drawing

In preparation for the drawing, first the vertical face is trowelled to ensure that it is as straight as possible. Next, a datum line, or base line, is created, from which to take measurements. At the top of the section, a string is nailed to one side of the ditch and stretched across to the other side . It is kept tight and a mini spirit level is used to make sure that it is perfectly horizontal and isn't catching on any protruding stone or potshard, before the other side of the string is nailed to the opposite side of the ditch. The site surveyor will provide EDM readings for the two ends of the datum string, which will need to be adjusted if they turn out not to be the same height – they should be the same height for the string to be absolutely level. A tape

measure can now be run along this string, attaching it to the nails with clips (not the string, or it will droop). This tape gives the horizontal scale for the drawing, and a hand tape measure can be used to take vertical readings above and below the string.

Making the drawing

To represent the string, one of the thicker lines on the graph paper is chosen, and to indicate it as the base line, arrows are drawn on either side of the section drawing. Next, the sides of the ditch are measured and drawn in in relation to the base line, with the measurements being transferred to the tracing paper by the means of dots

and then joining the dots to represent as accurately as possible the shape of the ditch sides.

The horizons of the layers that fill the ditch are then drawn, along with the stones of the culvert and the fill below and above. Larger inclusions, such as stones in the ditch fill, are also drawn in as accurately as possible. Finally, the drawing is labelled to show the context numbers that were allocated to each layer and feature as the ditch was excavated, along with the site and trench reference numbers, a note of the scale at which

Below A large, opened context is measured and recorded here with the aid of a crane.

Recording the stratigraphic layers of a context

1 The 'horizons' of each discernible level of the sides of the ditch are measured and readings noted.

2 Readings are then drawn to scale on graph paper and joined up to form a record of the stratigraphy.

the drawing has been made, the orientation (the direction in which the section is facing) and the digger's initials and date, to indicate who made the drawing in case questions need to be asked at a later stage. If stylized conventions are used to indicate differences in ditch fill – for example, dots to indicate gravel – a key also needs to be supplied.

Photography

As well as making a drawn plan of the site, a photographic record is maintained of the site at every stage in its excavation. This photographic record is a valuable additional check for future archaeologists who might want to use the site data. Some photographs are taken specifically as an integral part of the site record, along with the drawings, finds and context sheets. Others are taken to place features and the site as a whole into its wider context. It is also useful to have some general site shots taken during the course of the dig, including diggers at work. As well as being useful for future publications and for illustrating lectures, there is a great nostalgic value in being able to look back a decade or more hence on what will, hopefully, have been a memorable excavation.

If the site is large, photographing the site in its entirety is not always easy; if the director anticipates the need to gain a high view of the site, scaffolding towers or an elevated platform known as a 'cherry picker' can be rented and used for taking aerial views. Some archaeologists have tried attaching cameras to kites and helium balloons, but these are rarely as easy to control and manoeuvre as one might like. Aerial photographs of the site are a great bonus, and might be obtainable if there is an airstrip in the vicinity and light aircraft owners willing to fly over your site with a camera.

Film and digital

Although digital photography is now widely used, some archaeologists still use 35mm film, and the different requirements of site archives, publication and lectures means that some also like to take black-and-white pictures as well as colour.

Digital photography is increasingly used as the price of good quality digital cameras comes down. Digital cameras are also excellent for making a 'social' record of the site – especially for use in lectures and on websites because they are easily integrated into computer-based applications.

Shot composition

Lighting is critical for all site photography. The whole of the subject needs to be lit by the same light, not half in bright sunshine and the other in shade. It is also important that record shots taken of features and deposits or finds before they are removed from the ground have a scale and a north arrow.

The area to be photographed must be impeccably clean and free of debris, spoil, tools, labels, clothes, and so on – hence the sections are photographed last, after the section drawing has been completed and the section string, nails and labels have been removed. At the last moment the area to be photographed can be sprayed with water to enhance colours and contrasts.

Above After the site has been drawn, labels, pins and tapes are removed and the site cleaned for photography.

Revealing the Layers

The excavation of a site is an exciting time for archaeologists, but also a testing one. Having revealed in plan – that is in bird's eye view – what features appear to exist on the site, it is usual for the diggers to pause and think about a number of questions.

The key concepts that need to be addressed mainly relate to 'phasing' and 'stratigraphy' of the site. These concepts are central to all archaeology – they are the main analytical tools that we have for understanding the phases of activity that have taken place in the past on the site.

Phasing is a shorthand term for questions such as: how old are these features, are they all of one period, or do they represent several periods of activity? Can we put these features into some kind of relative chronological order, from the newest features on the site to the oldest? Can we tell whether these different phases of use were continuous and evolutionary, or were there periods of use and abandonment –

maybe seasonal (used in summer, not in winter), maybe separated by much longer periods of time?

Stratigraphy

Answering those questions is only possible if we can investigate the stratigraphy, a concept derived from geology that involves the analysis of the different layers found in soil sections. Geologists study sections that can be many metres deep and that represent millions of years of titanic geological processes, such as volcanic eruption, flooding and the deposition of sands and gravels, or the folding, heating and compression of rocks. Archaeologists tend to work with much smaller soil sections, which represent the smaller

Above On urban sites, the phasing is often complex due to repeated use through history.

chunks of time that result from small-scale human activity. Even so, the basic principles are the same, and they are based on the logical premise that the lowest layers in any section through the earth are the oldest and the highest ones are the most recent.

Phasing

Using this relatively basic concept, it is not difficult to understand the phasing of a simple ditch that has slowly filled from the bottom up. However, stratigraphic analysis is more complex when you begin to look at the intersections of two or more different

Above The layers of a cliffside context have been tagged in Wyoming, USA.

Left Recording a section through layers of peats and gravels at an intertidal location.

Cowdery's Down

No matter how carefully you prepare in advance, occasionally archaeology has the power to throw up something unexpected. At Cowdery's Down, in Hampshire, England, archaeologists turned up in the late 1970s to excavate what they thought from aerial photographs and trial excavation was the site of a Civil War fortification. They thought it was where parliamentary forces had set up gun platforms on the hillside to blast away at the Royalist-held Basing House on the opposite side of the valley, which would date the site to the mid-17th century. However, that guess was proven to be wrong by 1,000 years.

Once the site was opened up in full, archaeologists found a complete Saxon village – the first of its kind ever to be found in England – with a number of large hall houses, each sitting in its own fenced yard, amid a maze of ditches and pits. The challenge that then faced

Above The phasing at this Anglo-Saxon village was based on painstaking excavation of the post holes, representing the remains of fences and property boundaries.

the archaeologists was to answer the question: are these houses and other features all of the same date? The only way to tell was to look for the points where the post holes left by the rotten timbers of one house or fence cut through another. A very small number of such post holes were found, forming a sort of '8' shape rather than an 'O'. Delicate excavation of soil at the point where the two post holes met established which one was the oldest and which the newest of the two.

Archaeologist then used this critical stratigraphical evidence and correlated it with other evidence that was found at the site – slight differences in the alignments of the fences and huts, for example, or in the style of the construction, or in the internal layout – to phase the site's many different periods. Some of the ditches and fences were proven to be Iron Age and Roman, and the hall houses themselves were proven to have been rebuilt and replaced several times during the period from the late 5th to the early 8th century.

phases of activity. In an urban environment, for example, where people have lived on the same site for hundreds – or thousands – of years, adapting what they find or building new houses on top of old, the resulting stratigraphy is a mind-bending mix of deposits. Some will lie on top of others, some will cut through others, while some will abut others and some are entirely contained within others (this is called a lens).

Vital clues to the phasing of the site can be found in those superimpositions and juxtapositions of layers, some of which can be very slight and easily destroyed during excavation. It is perhaps the most difficult challenge any archaeologist faces, deciding where exactly to dig in order to find those critical diagnostic intersections that tell the story of the phasing of the site.

Left Deep contexts, such as this medieval well, provide a rich stratigraphic record.

The Site Matrix

Before a digger leaves a ditch after it has finally been excavated, it is essential to try to place the ditch itself within the wider context of the whole site, showing how it relates to the other features that have also been dug up and recorded.

Distinguishing between contexts and understanding their relationships can be the most challenging and difficult part of any excavation, because it is a matter of judgement and interpretation. Fortunately, establishing stratigraphical relationships does not need to be a solitary activity or a one-time event. Diggers are encouraged to discuss their thoughts with fellow diggers and supervisors – indeed, much of the conversation that takes place at the end of a long hard day over dinner or around the camp fire is about

the overall interpretation of the site and how the various pieces fit together. It is often the case that preliminary thoughts are revised over and over again, as more evidence begins to emerge that might help the digger move from tentative to firmer ground.

Creating a matrix

Understanding the site as a whole is made easier by the use of a series of conventions that were devised by the Bermuda-born archaeologist Ed Harris, while working on excavations

Above Chaotic as it looks, the site matrix will reduce this site to a clear chronological record.

in Winchester, England, in 1973. His set of conventions, known as the Harris Matrix, or (less often) the Winchester seriation diagram, are now used all over the world as a means of describing stratigraphy relationships. However, many other archaeologists were involved in refining the basic approach through work undertaken in Cirencester and in London during the 1970s and 1980s.

The matrix for any site will look like a family tree diagram, with boxes that have context numbers instead of people's names. The uppermost context is at the top – it represents the most recent deposit. Different types of feature are represented by different shaped boxes – to distinguish between deposits, cuts and hard features. In the case of a simple ditch, the diagram will show a basic linear progression, of one context lying over another. However, if another feature is encountered within the ditch – for example, a post hole cut into the fill of the ditch, with its own cut and fill – that would be shown as a separate branch off the main tree.

Floating and fixed matrices

The matrix for the ditch is a complete representation of the ditch and its fill, but it is floating without a wider context unless the ditch matrix is joined to a larger diagram of the site,

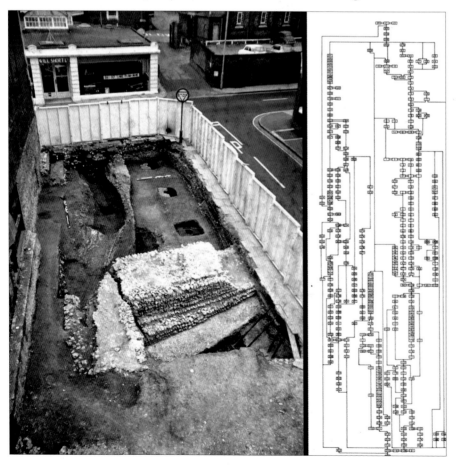

Left The extensive matrix to the right can be read by an archaeologist as a timeline of features at the Roman wall site on the left.

showing the relationships of every feature to another. This can be done only if a section of the ditch is found that cuts or is cut by another feature, enabling archaeologists to show a relationship between the two features. Bit by bit the floating matrices can be joined together like a jigsaw to create a phased matrix for the whole site; at least, in the ideal world, for it is one of the frustrating facts of archaeology that it is not always possible to define a clear physical relationship between one context and another, although similarities in the fill and in the finds from each context might suggest they belong to the same phase.

The example of the box culvert, right, shows how multiple contexts can be placed into a logical sequence.

Creating a Harris Matrix

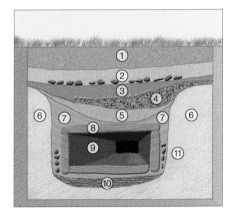

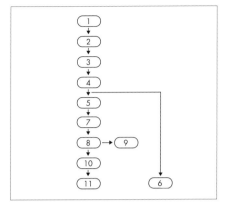

1 Every context has a number, including the cut itself (11), each number representing the physical counterpart to an event or action in the life of the culvert.

2 These events or actions are then represented in a chronological diagram, with recent events appearing at the top and the oldest events at the bottom.

The excavation record

The process that a digger will go through to excavate a ditch is one that quickly becomes familiar, and that will be repeated many times during the course of the excavation. Here is a quick summary of the basic steps:

- Clean the area to define the extent of the context
- Assign a number to the context
- Take photographs of the context
- Plan the context
- Survey the context to pinpoint its position
- Excavate the context and in doing so define the limits of the next context
- Recover artefacts (and environmental samples) from the context and record 'special' finds
- Describe the context on a recording sheet, including its physical relationship to other contexts
- Survey the context to give its height in relation to the site datum
- Repeat the process until the context has been excavated in its entirety
- Draw the resulting section

- Define and describe the 'cut' represented by the feature
- Survey in the base/natural layer of the feature.

Site archive

The collective result of this activity will be a set of data that records all the excavated material and that consist of:

- Notebooks listing all the site coordinates, context numbers, photographs, drawings, finds and special finds
- Plans and section drawings of the whole site as well as of individual contexts
- Context record sheets and matrices
- Black-and-white and colour photographs
- Finds and environmental samples.

All of the items in these lists are now familiar with the exception of the finds and the environmental samples. (*For more on these, see* Rich Finds and Humbler Finds.)

Below Excavating and recording is a repetitive activity, but the thrill of discovering and sharing knowledge of finds is never dull.

Case Study: Frocester Court

Frocester Court is the site of one of Britain's longest-running continuous excavations. Since 1961, enthusiasts have been excavating a 2.8-ha (7-acre) site with thorough and painstaking care in order to try and understand the 4,000-year history of Frocester parish, starting in the Bronze Age.

Above One of Frocester's Roman finds – the rim and base of a cooking jar dating from the 4th century.

Mr Eddie Price, the owner of Frocester Court, knew that there was something in the field opposite his farmhouse because there were stony areas that were difficult to plough, where he picked up a large amount of pottery. Mr Price showed the pottery to Captain Gracie, a local archaeologist, who visited Frocester in 1961, dug a trench and found a Roman mosaic pavement. Captain Gracie returned every year until 1978 when he became too ill to continue, and Mr Price took over as the director of excavations.

Frocester's story

The mosaic pavement turned out to be the floor of a long corridor running the length of a Roman villa, dating from the end of the 3rd century. However, careful excavation of the area around the villa made Mr Price realize that this was just one phase of the history of the site, and he made it his mission to excavate the field and gradually unpick the archaeology in order to follow the fortunes of human activity at Frocester right from first beginnings to the present day.

The Bronze Age

The earliest evidence that could be found at the site for human occupation was a well, with a timber post set in the centre – perhaps as a marker, perhaps used as a ladder. The post was radio-carbon dated to 1600BC, the early Bronze Age.

Typical early Bronze Age pottery was found in a territorial boundary ditch that ran for some 300m/985ft across the site, joining a hollow trackway. It was fenced on either side, so it was probably used as a droveway for moving cattle from site to site.

The Iron Age

By the Iron Age (from 700BC), the sunken droveway had been abandoned, but a new track has developed alongside it, leading to a very large enclosure surrounded by a 3m- (10ft-) deep ditch, perhaps filled with water like a moat. Within the enclosure were some large round buildings, as well as

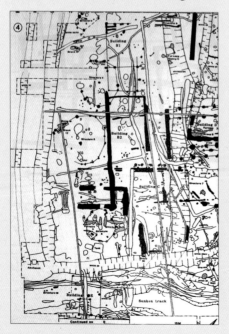

Left This plan of part of the site points out some of the early Roman buildings.

an elaborate arrangement of fences and stock pens, designed for sorting sheep or cattle into different groups. While humans and beasts co-existed happily inside the farmyard enclosure, there was also a large external garden area, deliberately kept separate from the farmyard to prevent animals trampling or eating the crops.

Toward the end of the Iron Age (say 200BC), the interior of the farm enclosure was divided up into smaller pens, which Mr Price thinks were for smaller animals – hens, pigs, sheep and goats – with rectangular granaries for storing grain. During the same time the external garden had grown to include arable fields. The round houses had been rebuilt even larger, with one main house and two smaller ones – perhaps the homes of an extended family or perhaps, Mr Price suggests, for the farmer and his two wives.

A beautiful bronze neck ring, or torque, was discovered in the foundations of the bigger house, perhaps placed there as a foundation offering. Other finds include horse bones and the moulds for casting the type of lynch pins found on Iron Age chariots, suggesting that the farmer was prosperous enough to own the equivalent of a luxury car.

Dramatic change

By AD100 the moated enclosure, the garden and fields were still there, however, the round houses and internal fences had been swept away and

Reconstructing the history of Frocester Court

Above This reconstruction draws on the earliest evidence from Frocester, and shows a Bronze Age track, wells and boundary ditch.

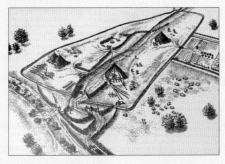

Above The enclosed site and large circular buildings of this phase characterize the early Iron Age farm.

Above By the late Iron Age, the round houses have grown in stature, and the interior has been subdivided into distinct 'pens'.

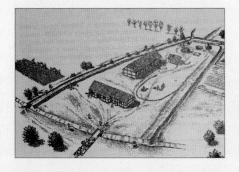

Above The first Roman farm of 100–275AD, with internal divisions removed and rectangular timbered buildings in place.

Above The grand Roman villa of Frocester Court was built in the 4th century AD, and was set among extended grounds.

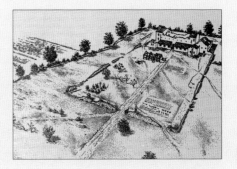

Above By the post-Roman phase the villa has declined, but the site continued to be farmed from the 5th century onward.

replaced by Roman-style rectangular buildings made of timber and thatch. Farming was still going on, but also some industrial activity, to judge from the iron and bronze working hearths.

By the 3rd century AD, the evidence suggests that the farm had become a larger estate, with the main centre of occupation elsewhere. Large numbers of 'goads' for guiding oxen were found from this period — evidence that oxcarts were used to bring the crops in from the fields. Behind one of the barns is a cemetery containing the remains of 40 infants — a sad reminder of the high rate of child mortality at this period.

Living in luxury

Some time in the last quarter of the third century the site ceased to be a working farmyard, and a substantial Roman style villa was constructed with massive walls, suggesting that it was several storeys high. Archaeologists found the evidence for the demolition

of the older barns, and for the first time in 1,000 years, the moat enclosing the site was filled in and the site appears to have expanded beyond its Iron Age limits.

About 100 years later, the villa was given a makeover and became even more luxurious, with underfloor heating, mosaic floors, a bath house, and a beautiful formal garden. All of this might well be evidence for the prosperity that might have occurred once Roman control of the countryside began to weaken.

After the Romans

Unfortunately, all good things must end. For a while, weaker Roman rule brought prosperity, and those good solid Roman roads meant that it was possible to take goods to markets in still-thriving towns. However, little by little, the infrastructure of late Roman Britain began to break down and life at the villa became more and more

impoverished. Refuse that was found in and around the villa suggests that fewer and fewer rooms were used, and there is evidence that parts of the villa were used to house animals. Within only two centuries, the grand villa was abandoned, robbed of useful building materials and ironwork, and parts were burned down. Even so, the site continued as a farm centre until being abandoned before *c.* 800AD in favour of the present estate centre and the developing Saxon village.

By the late 7th century the Roman villa had been entirely abandoned, and a new area of Saxon settlement had grown up in a different part of Frocester parish. As Frocester Court entered consecutive periods of open-field farming, the farmhouse that is on the site today was built during the 16th century, and a magnificent medieval barn constructed when Frocester was part of the estate owned by the monks of Gloucester Abbey.

RICH FINDS AND HUMBLER FINDS

It is reasonable to think that archaeologists are principally concerned with finding things, especially gold and silver jewellery, sculptures, pots full of coins or spectacular mummies and tombs because that is what is often displayed in museums. It is also what gets the media's attention; for example, the 25- to 30-year-old Anglo-Saxon woman found at Butler's Field in Gloucestershire, England, was nicknamed 'Mrs Getty' by the press because of the rich finds from her grave, whereas they ignored the graves of humbler people, which are just as interesting to archaeologists. Analysis of their teeth or bones can tell us what they ate, how old they were, what ailments they had and whether they were local people who adopted Saxon lifestyles or migrants from the Netherlands, Denmark or Germany. In fact, what interests an archaeologist is any material that can yield information. This chapter looks at the ingenious ways in which archaeologists extract knowledge from even the humblest of finds.

Opposite Pottery urns from a cremation cemetery in Languedoc-Rousillon, used from 11th–7th century BC.

Above The head of Archaeological Reserves of Ecuador examines a pre-Columbian statuette in a storage site in Quito.

Above Sandy deposits from the Çatalhöyük site in Turkey are sifted through a large circular mesh in the search for microscopic finds.

Above Microscopic remains of plants or charred earth are examined as part of the evidence-gathering process.

Artefacts and Ecofacts

Archaeological finds are broadly classified into two categories: artefacts that are the result of human craft, and ecofacts, which are of natural origin and help us understand the environment and landscape surrounding any site being studied. Different recovery and study methods apply to each category.

The excavation of an archaeological site involves the removal of layers of soil in the reverse order from that in which they were deposited, so arch-aeologists can understand the physical features of a site. Most of that soil gets left behind when the archaeologists depart, but not the finds that come from the soil. Instead, as the site is excavated, the digger will be expected to keep a sharp eye open for finds, which are removed from the soil, placed in a labelled tray and sent to the finds shed for further work.

What is a find?

What counts as a 'find' very much depends on the nature of the site and the recovery strategy that the site director has established. Some sites are so rich in finds that to take everything away for study would require a very large vehicle; these are called common, or bulk, finds. The ancient Roman buildings found all over Europe, the Mediterranean and North Africa are often constructed of durable materials, such as stone, brick and tile. Even if they were 'robbed' in the past by later people, who wanted to reuse the materials in their own structures, the mess and debris left by a collapsed or demolished Roman building is often substantial. In such cases, it is normal to keep a basic record of the quantity and weight of building material from the site, but to keep only examples that are special, because they are intact, or

Above Charred munitions found at the Roman settlement at Farafra, Egypt, which was fortified to protect the routes to other oases.

because the clay tile bears a manu-facturer's stamp, the maker's thumb print or some idly scratched graffiti.

By contrast, there are sites that are so insubstantial that every effort is taken to record and salvage the slightest find. Tracking down the camp fires of our earliest nomadic ancestors is a challeng-ing task in which no piece of evidence – even charcoal flecks, bone fragments and pollen – is taken for granted.

Below Palmyra in Syria, one of the most important Roman sites of the Middle East, is rich in architectural remains.

Above (clockwise from top) Carved wooden projectile point from the Hoko wet site; hafted microlith with green stone cutting edge, *in situ*; part of a stone bowl from the dry site.

The Hoko River archaeological site

A dramatic example of the way that environmental conditions can effect the survival rate of artefacts and ecofacts comes from the Hoko River Rockshelter and shell midden (a rubbish heap of shells), in Washington, an American site that straddles both dry land and wet land locations. The list of materials recovered from the waterlogged deposits, where the conditions preserve organic material, include baskets, hats, mats, fishing lines and nets, wooden fishhooks, needles and garment pins. We would know little about the life of the Hoko River people, or their fishing and weaving skills, if we only had the artefacts from the dry side, consisting largely of stone tools and blades.

pollens or identifying the species from which bone fragments have come requires years of training and familiarity with the material. Artefacts can be appreciated more easily for what they are because they correspond more directly with the everyday objects that we still use. Yet they also have a scientific side, because the microscopic inclusions in the clay in pottery, for example, can help pin down exactly where the pot was made and food residues on the sides or in the porous body of the vessel can tell us what the pot was used for.

No hard boundaries

These are all generalizations, of course, because there is no very hard boundary between artefact and ecofact – where, for example, does charcoal fit, a material modified by humans but also the by-product of natural processes, such as forest fires. In fact, arch-aeologists do argue among themselves about what exactly is natural and what is artificial, although one of the great achievements of archaeologists in recent years has been to extend hugely the amount of information that can be extracted from all types of find – and not just those that are freshly dug. Unravelling the diets of Bronze Age people from studying the chemistry of their tooth enamel, or reconstructing the DNA of Neanderthals from fossilized bones can bring new relevance to material stored away in archives from decades-old excavations.

Man-made or natural finds

The contrast between the Roman and the prehistoric site also highlights the two main types of find that archaeo-logists collect and study: typically referred to as 'artefacts' and 'ecofacts'.

Artefacts are objects that have been used, modified or made by humans. The ones archaeologists find tend to be of durable materials, such as stone, metal and ceramic, although frozen, arid and waterlogged sites might also yield artefacts made of organic materials, such as leather, wood, woven

straw or reed, paper and cloth. Ecofacts, by contrast, tend to be floral and faunal – that is, they consist of plant material, such as pollen, or of the remains of once-living organisms, such as snail shell or beetle wings.

Different techniques

Artefacts and ecofacts are often different in size. Whereas artefacts are usually visible to the naked eye, many ecofacts are so small that a microscope is needed for their study. This means that the collection strategy for each is different. Artefacts can be separated from the soil deposits in which they are found and are recoverable during the process of excavation or through sieving (sifting) through a coarse mesh. However, ecofacts are often recovered by means of soil sampling; the soil is then washed and filtered through a fine mesh – sometimes in an on-site laboratory, and sometimes away from the site at a later date.

Artefacts and ecofacts are often studied in different ways, too. Ecofacts in particular are the realm of the trained scientist, often using laboratory equipment, such as microscopes and spectrometers, where classifying

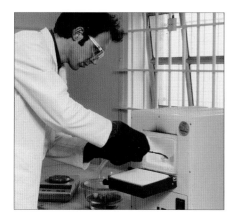

Above Preparation of samples during soil and sediment analysis.

Above Excavating a relatively modern lime kiln from the 18th–19th century.

Processing Finds on Site

As finds are recovered from the archaeological site, they are taken to the finds shed or an on-site laboratory for processing. Here, finds are logged, inspected, cleaned and perhaps given emergency conservation treatment before they are stored for future study.

The task of running the finds lab is usually entrusted to a specialist with some knowledge of basic conservation practice. However, on a busy site there can be more finds than one person can cope with, and this is where volunteers are often able to help, taking a day off from digging to learn what happens to finds when they reach the finds shed.

Much finds work is routine and repetitive. By long-established tradition, archaeologists usually store finds in plastic trays, buckets or paper bags.

Below Common finds are placed in a labelled tray to be cleaned; special finds are bagged and their precise find spot recorded.

A popular option among British archaeologists is a shallow rectangular kind of plastic tray that gardeners often use for seed propagation.

Diggers are given a new finds tray at the beginning of every day. One key task is to ensure that every tray has a waterproof label with the site code and context number written on it so that there is a record of where the finds have come from. Those same diggers hand in their finds trays at the end of every day, or when they are full. The person receiving the trays must check that the labels are still intact and have not been mislaid or blown away – if so, they will require relabelling.

Above These pieces of pottery found at the Constantinople excavations in Istanbul, Turkey, will stand up to robust cleaning, but other finds are much more vulnerable.

Cleaning finds

The finds handed in at the end of the previous day now require sorting and cleaning. Once it was common practice to clean every find thoroughly in water and detergent, perhaps using a toothbrush or nailbrush to remove stubborn mud or stains. However, today there is an increasing awareness that the cleaning process can destroy vital evidence, such as food residues sticking to the surfaces of unglazed cooking pots or absorbed by the porous body of an earthenware storage jar, or soot from the cooking process that can be carbon dated. Overzealous cleaning can wash away bloodstains, paint, pigments, fabric, wood and other organic remains, and one scientist has recently warned archaeologists that they risk losing vital DNA evidence if they immerse bones in water.

Consequently, the site director will decide on a general strategy for salvaging and cleaning finds, in consultation with the finds supervisor. The decision about what to wash, what

Below A puppy's paw-print made on the drying clay of a Roman roof tile.

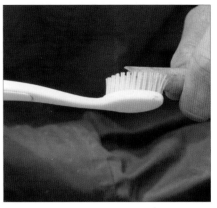

Above The soft bristles of a toothbrush are ideal for cleaning flint and bone.

Above The find is bagged, labelled and pinned to the spot where it was found so that it can, in due course, be plotted on the site plan.

to keep and what to weigh, measure and discard, will depend on the type of site and the type of finds and what sort of evidence the finds can reasonably be expected to yield.

How much to keep?

In an ideal world, everything from the site should be kept. In reality, the costs of storing and studying what are known as 'common finds' or 'bulk finds' can be so great that a balance has to be struck between the investment of time and money and the likely result in terms of information.

Often a decision is made by the director to keep just a sample of the finds, selecting material that is more likely to prove significant or diagnostic in the interpretation and understanding of the site. This strategy can be justified on the grounds that any excavation is, by definition, a sampling exercise. Rarely does an archaeologist get the opportunity to dig a site in its entirety, so the finds from one stretch of ditch are already just a random selection of a small percentage of the artefacts that might have survived.

However, archaeologists have a habit of discovering new ways of extracting information from finds that were once regarded as uninformative. Because of this, some archaeologists increasingly opt for the 'just in case'

strategy of keeping everything — although this can cause a major storage problem in due course.

Where bulk finds are not kept, they are still washed and laid out to dry in the sunshine, usually on old newspaper. Washing or gentle brushing removes mud that might conceal details that can elevate the find to a higher category. Roman roof tiles are routine and utilitarian objects, but occasionally one will have an animal footprint — made by a dog, for example, that has stepped

onto the drying clay while it was still soft enough to take a paw print. Such marks are popular in museum exhibits or as educational material, because they help to bring the past to life.

Bulk finds are then counted, weighed and described before being discarded. A good strategy is to bury them in a place on the site where they are likely to be undisturbed and to record the burial site in the site archive, so that future archaeologists can go back and recover them if a future need arises.

Above The southern gate of the Roman remains at Silchester, near the town of Reading, UK, has been continually excavated since the 19th century, and the site tells us as much about past excavations as about the settlers who built the town.

Going back at a later date

Bulk finds that are reburied at the end of a dig will lose their context and provenance, so they are of less value to future archaeologists. However, they do not entirely lose their value as a source of information. Archaeologists excavating the Roman town of Silchester, in central southern England, have been exploring the dumps left in 1893.

By analysing the contents of the pits, archaeologists were able to develop an insight into the excavation techniques and retrieval strategies of their 19th-century predecessors, learning, for example, what type and proportion of finds had been kept for further study and what was discarded. The pit contents also gave an insight into the range of refreshments that were consumed on site (mineral water, whisky and beer from Amsterdam) and even from which local baker and pastry cook they obtained some of their food supplies.

Activity in the Finds Shed

When a volunteer is asked to help in the finds shed for the day, the finds supervisor will explain the routine and some of the basic principles for dealing with finds. The routine will consist of sorting, packing and labelling the finds, all of which are important in keeping accurate records.

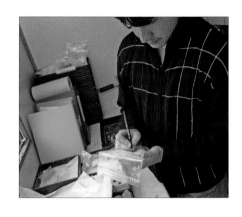

At the start of the day, the find supervisor will ask a volunteer to line up all the finds trays from the previous day's excavation, so that the director and site supervisors can review what has been found. Supervisors can easily become detached from what is happening on other parts of the site, so ideally the director will hold a meeting – perhaps at the beginning or the end of the day – where everyone can review progress on the site as a whole.

The supervisors also constantly monitor the finds that come out of features as they are excavated, because this is primary information that affects the interpretation of the site and the excavation strategy. In addition, special finds – in particular any finds that might help with the dating of features on the site (*see* Finds in Context) – are looked at as soon as they are found.

Below Finds are reviewed daily because they give clues to the interpretation and dating of the features being excavated.

Reviewing and comparing

By reviewing the finds, the supervisors can spot patterns and anomalies. For example, whether or not the various pits in different parts of the site have the same type of finds or different ones – perhaps more or less bone, or bone of different types of animal. Each of the supervisors may have a different area of expertise. The pottery expert can share his or her thoughts on the dating and significance of the pottery from the site, while a zooarchaeologist, who specializes in animal bone, can give a view on the meaning of the material that is found. Does it represent one animal type or many, one cut of meat, such as leg bones, or whole carcasses, are the bones from young or mature animals? The answers to these and other questions all provide information about the site.

Below Archaeology students are shown how to remove particles of earth clinging to the fragments of human skulls.

Above All these special finds are entered into a register to ensure that they do not get lost.

Sorting and packing finds

Once the team meeting has finished, the volunteer's task will be sorting the previous day's finds into different materials. Robust finds are bagged by context and according to type – so all the pottery, for example, from context 901 is put into one bag, all the shell into another, all the bone into a third, and so on.

Strong paper bags are generally used for this purpose, but the volunteer might also be asked to use resealable plastic bags, which come in a variety of sizes and, most importantly, have perforations punched into them. These holes allow moisture to escape, rather than being trapped in the bag. This is vital to the integrity of the find because moisture can cause unstable objects to corrode or crumble, and it encourages mould to form, damaging the material beyond repair.

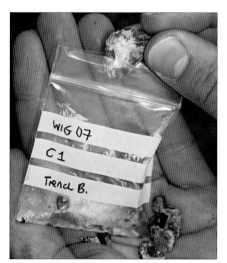

Right Here, the animal bones from an excavation are carefully sorted by type and context.

Labelling

The finds supervisor is obsessive about labelling everything – not just once, but twice. First, the volunteer will be asked to write the site code, trench number and context number on the outside of the bag using a waterproof permanent marking pen – resealable plastic bags sometimes have white panels specifically designed for being written on by a pen – and then the volunteer places a waterproof label into the bag with the finds. So the pottery found in a ditch yesterday (*see* Finds in Context) is labelled with the site code AHF07 (*see* Preparing to Dig a Section), the trench code Trench 9 and a code (901) for the context or locus, along with the date when the finds were made.

Finds from different contexts in the same trench are kept together, usually in large stackable plastic boxes. The volunteer should put heavy and robust finds at the bottom of the box and more delicate finds at the top, thereby avoiding delicate pottery being crushed by heavy tile or brick.

Breaking the routine

The bagging and labelling can become a boring routine, but sometimes the routine is broken. For example, one of the supervisors might come into the finds shed to report that a coin has been found. Archaeologists love coins because they can help with the dating of site features. To everyone's disappointment, the finds supervisor insists that nobody rubs the coin to remove the green corrosion covering the coin's surface, because this can damage the coin (*see* Vulnerable Finds).

Instead, the spot where the coin was found is recorded (*see* Finds in Context) and the coin is given a unique find number, which is recorded in the finds log and written on the context sheet, so that everyone will know that special find number 85 came from context 179, and that it came from this very specific spot on the earth.

Although the significance of its precise location will be unknown at the time, it is worthwhile recording the details carefully in case future digging reveals other artefacts that are associated with the special find.

Archaeologists always work on the principle of recording everything because you never know what information can be useful in the future – and it is impossible to travel back in time if you don't record something.

Above The discovery of this Roman copper cauldron is rare because metals were often melted down and reused.

Special finds

In some parts of the world, special finds are called 'archaeological objects' – however, neither term is satisfactory because all finds are archaeological objects and 'special' is a subjective term (*see* Finds in Context), and archaeologists, as scientists, try not to use value-laden words. Whatever they are called, they can have a legal dimension. Some countries will not permit the export of archaeological objects of a certain age or type, so if a visiting archaeological team is studying and conserving such finds, the work must be done in the host country. There can also be a legal duty to report such finds to a local museum or antiquities authority.

Vulnerable Finds

Common finds, such as tile, brick and stone, tend to be durable and robust, so they do not need special care. However, many finds are more delicate and will need proper first-aid treatment if they are to be preserved from damage for further study.

Once they are taken out of the ground, finds that have enjoyed stable conditions for centuries – if not thousands of years – will suddenly undergo a dramatic change in their environment. Woken from their long sleep, finds can undergo rapid deterioration when exposed to the air, sunlight and the physical handling of a curious sweaty-palmed archaeologist. In fact, these finds would probably shriek with pain if they had nerves and senses.

Minimal handling

Another key principle with all finds is to minimize how much they are handled. Depending on what type of site a volunteer is working on, this principle might even extend to a ban on handling finds with bare hands or on using sharp tools for excavation or cleaning. On a waterlogged site, for example, where wood can survive but might have the texture and consistency of a sponge cake, plastic spatulas are used to handle the finds, and surgical gloves are worn at all times.

Metal is especially vulnerable to decay from handling, so no matter how strong the desire is to clean the corrosion from the surface of that newly discovered coin to see how old it is, the urge has to be resisted. Rubbing the surface damages the patina – the

stable layer of corrosion that covers the surface. Removing this exposes the uncorroded metal beneath and starts the corrosion process all over again, so that important details, such as the lettering of an inscription or the mark of the mint where the coin was made, can be lost.

How rapidly finds deteriorate will depend on the nature of the material from which they are made and how great the contrast is between their buried environment and the one to which they are newly exposed. The greatest harm comes from the desiccation of materials that were previously wet or damp, and vice versa – for example, atmospheric moisture causing corrosion to metal objects. Therefore, the aim is to try to replicate

Above Slipware dish dating from the early–mid 16th century is excavated with great care.

the atmosphere from which the finds have just come, or to provide an alternative environment that is better for the finds.

Dry materials

Because damp and humidity can cause metals to decay, a coin will be allowed to air dry naturally (in a secure place) for 24 hours. The same treatment is good for all metal finds, including iron, copper, bronze, lead, tin and pewter. Finds made of these metals might well be brittle, so after drying out, they are laid on a supporting bed of crumpled-up acid-free tissue paper, in a rigid polystyrene box. The box is packed

Right Some finds are too delicate to excavate on site, where microscopic evidence would be missed. Instead, such finds are lifted from the site as a block of soil which is protected from damage by a plaster of Paris wrapping. The find is then transported to a laboratory for detailed examination.

Above Iron Age bronze shears, probably used for cutting textiles, with their carved container which is made from ash. The container also held a whetstone used for sharpening the shears. These finds were conserved at Flag Fen, UK, using a freeze-drying process.

Above A wooden barge from 100BC is found in the middle of a Netherlands town. It was once used to supply a Roman military base.

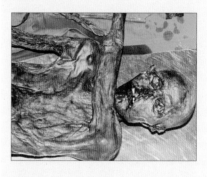

Above The well-preserved remains of Ötzi the Iceman are stored in a freezer.

with roughly the same weight of silica gel as the object weighs, along with a relative humidity indicator card, which has a coloured scale that reacts to damp. The relative humidity needs to be maintained at less than 15 per cent, which is achieved by sealing the box tightly, and checking at regular intervals, so that the silica gel bags can be replenished if necessary.

Silver and gold are stable metals, but they are rarely found as solid objects. More often one of these precious metals is applied as an outer layer to another material, such as wood, which might have deteriorated, or as gilding. In each case, the metal is likely to be thin and fragile and it too needs supporting and protecting from any external pressure.

The only exception is where it is thought that preserved organic remains are attached to a metal object – for example, a bone or wood handle to a knife, or leather or textile bindings. In this case, the object should be treated as if it were damp, and conservation advice sought immediately.

Damp and wet materials

By contrast, rapid drying is the enemy of materials that have ancient traces of paint – wall plaster, painted stone and sculpture, for example – or of natural materials, such as worked bone, wood,

ivory, shale, jet or amber, or the kind of fragile pottery that has been fired at a low temperature and that crumbles or breaks easily. Here, the aim is to maintain moisture levels by packing them with wet foam in a plastic box that has a tightly sealed lid.

Objects that are excavated from a waterlogged environment need more than damp foam to maintain moisture levels. They should be stored in a sealed box in distilled water to exclude atmospheric oxygen. Both damp and wet items should be refrigerated if possible – and they should certainly be kept cool and out of the sun to help prevent mould growth.

Wet finds

Flag Fen, near Peterborough, in eastern England, is a Bronze Age site, excavated from 1982, that produced very large quantities of well-preserved timber, so a special facility was built for preserving wet finds. Once excavated, the finds were placed in large tanks, where they were soaked in a solution of water and a wax called polyethylene glycol. It takes several years of immersion for the wax to fill the porous structure of the wood, after which the object can be slowly dried. The wax provides the support that prevents the object from shrinking or cracking as it dries.

Frozen finds

Occasionally archaeologists find frozen environmental evidence in permafrost, glaciers or on mountain tops, where the ground temperature never rises above freezing point. Spectacular discoveries from cold environments include the remains of humans, including the 5,300-year-old body of Ötzi the Iceman, found emerging from a melting glacier in the Italian Alps in 1991, and the 'Ice Maiden'. She was a 12- to 14-year-old girl apparently sacrificed by Inca priests on top of Mount Ambato near Arequipa in the Peruvian Andes in about 1480 – her frozen and well-preserved body was discovered in 1995. In both cases, the bodies were preserved by maintaining the cold conditions that had prevented the normal decay process, storing the remains at a maximum of -6°C (21°F).

Environmental Finds

One of the biggest changes in archaeological practice of the last few decades is the realization that sites contain far more finds than can be seen with the naked eye. These finds are recovered by taking and processing samples of the material from pits, ditches and other landscape features.

Biological or environmental remains are capable of telling archaeologists about many aspects of a site that they might not be able to deduce from more obvious finds. In particular, these remains are valuable for casting light on the type of environment that prevailed at the time the site was in use. Remember that landscapes change with use and weather patterns vary, with much still to be learned about their cycles. So although the archaeological site that is being excavated today might be in the middle of a grassy field surrounded by farmland, the scene might well have looked different in the past, and environmental remains can help provide clues to that past.

Past environments and weather

Pollens, plant remains, snail shells and insects are all materials capable of being used as evidence for reconstructing the environment at the time that the site was in use. Large amounts of tree pollen, for example, can indicate that the site was surrounded by woodland – perhaps it occupied a woodland clearing. The type of pollen and its relative abundance can also tell archaeologists whether the trees were being deliberately managed as coppice – that can be the case where hazel and willow pollen predominates, by contrast with a mixed woodland of oak, ash, alder, birch and so on.

Above Wet sieving stony earth for small finds and environmental evidence.

Some pollens are more indicative of grassland, or wetland environments (reeds and aquatic plants), just as many insects have specific habitat requirements and can thus tell archaeologists whether the environment was wet, dry, wild or cultivated. In wetland sites, plant and insect remains can further refine the picture of the past by telling archaeologists whether the site was on an ancient coastline, estuary, river, lake or pond. The sensitivity of some plants and insects to specific climatic conditions can also fill in a picture of the prevailing weather,

Above Peat cores are extracted from the Bogwater Copse in the Sandhills of North Carolina, as part of a project to reconstruct the hunter-gatherer history of this location. Pollens from surrounding vegetation were also sampled.

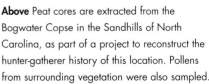

Left Students scan sifted soil looking for environmental plant and soil remains. The white background of the tray makes this easier.

which has long been a very important influence on human survival, migration and activity.

Economic information

Environmental remains can also give archaeologists an insight into the economy of the site, and the way that the people who lived there made use of their environment. Plant, bone, food and insect remains can, for example, demonstrate what types of crops were grown, what types of animals were kept and eaten, and whether the site was a smallholding, or a larger-scale farm, for example, processing pigs on an industrial scale.

These remains can tell archaeologists what type of diet the inhabitants enjoyed – whether, for example, it included wild foods, fish or shellfish, or even exotic imported foods from an entirely different part of the world. The remains can also tell archaeologists something about the health of the animals and humans – this information can be determined from the remains of insects and parasites.

One further and vital use for environmental remains is to provide material that can be used for dating parts of the site. Material that is suitable for carbon dating – such as wood, charcoal or plant material – is often obtained as a result of environmental sampling.

Right Durable remains, such as discarded oyster shells, are an excellent source of evidence of ancient diets.

Below These marigold seed cases, or 'burs', tell archaeologists about the ancient weeds and plant life of the site.

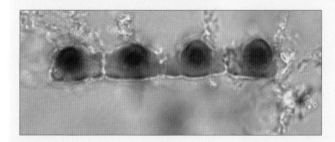

Above The phytoliths of these banana leaves are 'volcano-shaped', and distinguishable from those of a related genus on account of their specific physical form.

The first bananas in Africa

Soil samples have recently been used to trace the origin and spread of bananas from their botanical place of origin in New Guinea, where they were cultivated as early as 5000BC. Bananas do not preserve well, but it is possible to detect their presence through the study of phytoliths. These are microscopic particles produced by plants through interaction with minerals in the soil. They are commonly formed from silicon or calcium – hence their name (*phytolith* means 'plant stone'). The shape of the phytolith is unique to the plant, so it is easy to tell the difference between banana and strawberry phytoliths, for example. As minerals, they survive for a long time and can be dated using carbon-dating techniques.

Looking for phytoliths in soil samples from around the Indian Ocean, scientists at California State University in San Bernardino have established that bananas reached India and Pakistan by 3000BC, probably via Vietnam and Thailand. From India they quickly reached Africa: banana phytoliths have been found near the Uganda–Rwanda border dating from 3000BC. The implication is that Indian Ocean trading was already established by this date. We also know that African crops spread in the opposite direction, because sorghum and millet, cereal grains of the traditional African diet, had reached Korea by 1400BC.

Sampling Strategy

To decide how much material to save, the site director and site supervisors have to consider what sorts of deposits are most likely to yield well-preserved environmental materials. They then attempt to develop a logical sampling strategy appropriate to the site they are excavating.

The term 'bulk sample' is usually used to describe large samples taken away from a site and examined for environmental evidence in the laboratory. The material sampled in this way can include soil, hearth contents, peat and wood, and mineralized deposits, such as tufa – the calcium carbonate deposit that forms around springs, cisterns and wells, similar to the limescale that forms in hard-water areas.

Bulk samples can range in size from 10 litres (2½ gallons) – a bucketful – to as much as 100 litres (26½ gallons). This is a large amount of material to process, and sampling every context without a clear reason would not be a good use of limited resources.

If a site is thought to be rich in ecofacts, or environmental finds, an environmental specialist may be included as part of the excavation team. Bulk samples can then be processed on site, using sieves (screens) and flotation tanks (*see* Processing Soil Samples). This allows the environmental archaeologist to quickly identify where the best results are being obtained, so that the scale of the sampling can be increased accordingly and the maximum amount of material can be recovered.

The alternative is to seek specialist advice before the dig starts and agree to a site sampling strategy based on such factors as the likely survival rates of different kinds of environmental

Above Phytoliths are also found in artefacts made of plant matter. At the ancient site of Çatalhöyük in Turkey, samples were taken from baskets buried with the dead.

remains, given the geology of the site and the type of site that it is. The initial strategy should be regularly reviewed in the light of the material that is found as the dig progresses.

What survives where

The background geology might be favourable or hostile to the survival of ecofacts. For example, fewer environmental remains survive in acidic conditions than in alkaline or neutral ones. Charred deposits (the remains of

Above These pottery 'wasters' (a term referring to flawed pottery), found in a 2nd century AD pit, will provide a useful source of mineral evidence.

Left This grave site has an enormous amount of archaeological matter, from large and small finds to organic remains.

hearths, kilns or grain drying activity) yield valuable charcoals and charred plant remains, but destroy insect remains, pollens, spores and plant remains. Waterlogged deposits are the best for the survival of all types of organic material, followed closely by the type of soils that result from an accumulation of human or animal manure – what archaeologists politely call 'cess'. By contrast, fine silt contains fewer organic remains because the alluvial soil formation process leaves behind the heavier biological materials and deposits only fine clay particles.

The sampling strategy should also consider an evaluation of the probable types of feature that will be found on site. Bulk samples will always be taken from burials and cremation sites, if only because of the possibility of recovering small artefacts or artefact fragments that might help with the dating of the burials. Samples are also taken from bone-rich deposits to ensure that all bone is recovered, including smaller bones and fragments. (*For more on excavating human remains, see* The Study of Human Remains.)

Below Analysis of human remains reveals much about diet and disease.

Samples for reconstructing the economy of the site will be taken from any feature thought to be a floor surface, because this is where archaeologists hope to find microscopic debris from any occupational or industrial activities that took place on that floor. Samples from storage pits can tell us what was stored in them, and refuse pits are a gold mine for archaeologists, as are cess pits, middens (ancient refuse heaps), wells and moats.

For environmental reconstruction, the best sources for plant, insect and snail remains are ditches, buried turf lines, peat and the fill of water channels and gulleys, watering holes and ponds.

Environmental controls

As well as collecting material that will be used for working out what the climate and vegetation was like in the past, environmental archaeologists will also collect material from the current environment to provide comparative data. One way to do this is to dig holes around the site being excavated just large enough to hold a plastic drinking cup. The cups are inspected regularly to see what insects fall into the trap, and after counting and identification, they are released. The data collected in this

way will tell archaeologists what types of insects are at home in the ecological niche provided by the present environment, for comparison with the material from excavated samples. Material from the uppermost (or the most recent) layers might be similar in its insect life, while earlier layers might differ. If the archaeologist is lucky, it might be possible to identify the precise contexts in which the transition from, say, a woodland to a grassland environment took place, and perhaps even provide a date based on the site stratigraphy and phasing.

Above Samples were taken from the clay sediments using a 40cm (16in) long plastic down- (drain-) pipe, with the back cut off. They were later analysed for organic content.

The lions in the Tower
A plan to put water back into the moat surrounding the Tower of London was considered in the mid 1990s. As part of the feasibility study, archaeologists excavated sections of the moat. Among the remains they found were the bones of lions, bears and other exotic animal species, dating from the reign of King John (1199–1216) and confirming documentary references to his Royal Menagerie – medieval London's first zoo.

Soil Sampling Techniques

Although it might appear that taking a soil sample is a simple and straightforward procedure – as easy as shovelling earth into a bucket – this is often not the case. Different techniques are necesssary, depending on the nature of the material being sampled.

There are several different types of sample. Bulk sampling and column sampling are the two most likely to be entrusted to a volunteer – monolith and Kubiena samples (*see* Special Recovery Techniques) are the realm of the trained specialist.

The most common approach is single context sampling, where material is extracted from one context (unlike column sampling, where samples are taken from a sequence of related deposits). With single context sampling, care has to be taken to ensure that the sample is representative of the context it comes from. It must be taken from a part of the deposit that is free from potential contamination from surrounding layers or modern activity.

Below To ensure consistency in recording soil colour, a geological soil colour chart is used as a reference.

How much to take

The amount of material taken from the context will depend on various factors. Environmental archaeologists say that the finds from one standard bucket full of soil (a 10-litre (2½-gallon) sample) are statistically valid – they are typical of the feature as a whole. Even so, they recommend taking four buckets (40 litres (10 gallons)) of material.

If there are facilities on site for assessing the presence or absence of biological remains, a 10-litre (2½-gallon) sample is processed at once, and a further 30 litres (7½ gallons) retrieved if the first sample is positive. In the absence of such facilities, 40 litres (10 gallons) are taken, but when the time comes to process the sample, 10 litres

Below Peat bogs often take centuries to form and may be rich in evidence of past climates and ancient vegetation.

Above Boreholes are drilled on a river plain to extract samples of ancient river sediments.

(2½ gallons) will be assessed, and if the results are negative, the remaining material will be discarded.

Sometimes the deposit is slight, in which case the archaeologist might aim for 100 per cent recovery, even if it is less than the recommended minimum sample size of 10 litres (2½ gallons). In particular, this might be the case for a deposit that has been chosen for sampling because it is important in understanding the development, sequencing or dating of the site, such as a layer of burnt material in the fill of a ditch or pit, which could contain material suitable for carbon-14 dating, or that might represent the remains of a cremation, and could contain fragments of dateable material, such as glass beads or brooch fragments.

Left It is vital to record as much information as possible about the origins of ecofinds, in order to build a picture of the natural environment.

Right An example of an Environmental Sample Sheet as used by the Museum of London Archaeology Service. It is designed to be self-explanatory so that volunteers and inexperienced archaeologists can record samples fully and accurately for further investigation and interpretation.

ENVIRONMENTAL SAMPLE SHEET					
Area / Grid square	ENVIRONMENTAL SAMPLE		Site Code	Context	Sample no
Context type					
Provisional period or date (if known):					
Condition of deposit:	waterlogged	moist		dry	
Any contamination? eg	root action		mixture with overburden		
describe other:					
Sample volume (one sample tub = 10 litres):					
Sample size as proportion of entire context (tick):					
<5%	5–20%	20–40%	40–60%	60–80%	80–100%
Soil/sediment description:					
1. Compaction 2. Colour 3. Composition 4. Inclusions – indicate whether artefactual, biological or geological, and occa / mod / freq 5. Other comments					
Stratigraphic matrix					
NB transfer sample ASAP		This context is			
Specific questions about the sample (what do you want to know about the deposit?): eg: What biological remains are present? What are the characteristics of this assemblage? What was the function of this feature? What were the local environmental conditions like? Was it waterlogged?					
Are any subsamples required from this sample			yes	no	
radiocarbon	control sediment	parasites	insects	pollen	
diatoms	other (specify)				
Any related sample numbers eg	multi-sampled contexts		columns of samples		
(in latter case give sample dimensions):					
Sample taken by / date			Checked by / date		

© MUSEUM OF LONDON

However, an archaeologist might aim for a larger sample of a deposit that appears to be particularly rich in environmental remains – a judgement based on visual criteria, such as the presence of larger biological remains (charred grain or charcoal, for example) or its colour and composition (black, organic and peaty), or from its character as a floor bottom, hearth or pit-edge deposit.

What to take

Although purists might argue that soil samples should be truly representative of the deposit, in reality, there isn't much point in keeping non-diagnostic pebbles or stones, so those should be discarded (once entered on the context record sheets, plans and sections), and

Above Smaller samples should be bagged and labelled with information relating to site, date and context, and placed with the bulk deposits taken from the same location.

all artefactual finds should also be removed and treated as finds, rather than as part of the environmental sample.

Sample recording sheets

Soil samples are recorded using sample recording sheets and a sample register. As well as fixing the location and character of the sample, it should state why the sample was taken and from where, and what questions the sample might answer about the site or feature from which it came. These notes can affect the way the sample is processed in the laboratory. A distinction needs to be made between samples collected from occupational deposits that might have material evidence of people and their activities, and material from environmental deposits, where the aim is to understand the natural environment and exclude human debris.

It is also useful to estimate the size of the deposit and what percentage of the total deposit the sample represents. Fixing the precise location of the samples is important, especially when they have been taken from different points across a floor surface to see whether the finds can determine the segregation of different activities within the building – were specific parts used for food preparation, for example?

Finally, samples are labelled. One waterproof label is placed inside the bag/bucket with the site code, date, square/trench code, locus/context number, sample number (from the sample register) and type of sample. Another label, with the same information, is taped to the outside of the sample bucket, or placed in a plastic bag and tied to the handle.

The magic of metalwork

Evidence for early ironwork was recovered in bulk samples taken from two roundhouses at a site in Berkshire, southern England. Pottery and radiocarbon dating confirmed the site as a Late Bronze Age settlement of the 10th century BC. When the samples were later analysed, they were found to contain thousands of tiny metal fragments of a type known as hammerscale, which is the waste material created when raw iron is hammered to remove slag from the ore-smelting process, or when the metal is repeatedly heated and hammered to produce wrought iron.

By studying the concentrations of hammerscale in the soil, it was possible to work out precisely where in each roundhouse this work was taking place. Furthermore, it provided clear evidence that iron was being produced in the Late Bronze Age. The ironworking huts were located in a separate area from the main settlement, screened by an almost solid fence of closely spaced posts. Perhaps these prehistoric metalworkers were trying to ensure that no-one else witnessed their 'magical' transformation of rocks into metal.

Special Recovery Techniques

There are several methods of taking bulk soil samples. One involves extracting a whole vertical column of material, thus preserving the precise stratigraphy, others involve taking a carefully controlled sample of every layer in a series of deposits, to preserve the precise relationships of different soils for analysis.

Above Washed samples are dried in a heated cabinet before being examined.

Single-context samples are typically taken from selected contexts, such as floor surfaces or the primary (the earliest) fills of pits or ditches, because it is here that archaeologists expect to find the best evidence for the site when it was in use. However, sometimes it is useful to take samples from every deposit in a ditch or from a section through a feature. These will allow archaeologists to study the changes that have occurred over time.

Environmental interest

Not all features are suitable for this type of approach, but environmental archaeologists are particularly keen on finding deep sections that can result from long sequences of natural or human deposition, where the biological remains can potentially provide information on changes in culture or the environment over hundreds of years. They also love soils and turf lines that have been buried and preserved by later sedimentation or activity, because these can tell archaeologists what the environment was like immediately prior to the event that resulted in the burial of the soil.

Continuity or transition

Sometimes the story told by deep deposits is one of continuity and the absence of change. Sometimes, by contrast, the story is one of abrupt change or of gradual transition. For example, the earthen bank of a fortification or enclosure might be constructed on top of the existing turf, thereby preserving environmental data from the moment of the construction, which can be used to compare with later data. Such comparisons become especially relevant if, for example, the fortification was constructed by invaders – say, Roman conquerors of an Iron-Age territory in mainland Europe, or European colonialists arriving in the Americas, Australia, Canada, India or New Zealand. The buried soils thus potentially capture a moment of transition from one economy or set of lifestyles to another, and the study of the impacts of one culture on another are what academic archaeologists strive to understand.

Above Environmental samples are examined in a laboratory, with the aid of identification tools.

Left Archaeologists removing cores from a sea bed in an area that once existed as dry, inhabited land during the Mesolithic period.

Monoliths and Kubienas

Where suitable sections are found that fulfil these various criteria, there are two possible methods for salvaging material: one is to use monolith or Kubiena-type boxes, which are simply devices made by different manufacturers for collecting an intact block of soil without disturbing its structure. Made of brass, zinc or tin, like long rectangular bread or cake tins (typically 500mm (20in) in length, 140mm (5½in) in width and 100mm (4in) in depth). Many research digs abroad actually manufacture the similar sampling receptacles from locally available food canisters, although specially manufactured tins have the advantage of handles to enable their removal from the section complete with the soil block inside.

The tins are pushed into the exposed section or banged in using a rubber hammer. Several tins are used for deep sections. Each tin is numbered in sequence, and the tins are overlapped by 50mm (2in) or so, to ensure that a complete column is sampled without gaps. This method works best in softer soils, such as peat, where the tins can be cut out. However, the tins often have to be dug out of the section using a sharp spade to slice through the soil at the open end of the tins, which are then tightly wrapped to ensure that the soil block remains intact. After removal, the tins are carefully labelled.

Columns

The second sampling method does not require pre-manufactured tins – this is the columnar method, where accurately measured blocks of sediment are cut from each deposit using a trowel. The aim is to collect a sample size of 250mm (10in) x 250mm (10in) x 60mm (2⅜in), but the depth and thickness can vary, according to the nature of the deposit. The result from columnar sampling is a series of discrete samples, and although the relationships with adjacent deposits are not preserved, they are recorded on paper. Depending on the soil type, the sample might break up during extraction and storage, so some vertical information is lost as a result of mixing. However, the method is still effective for sampling layers of particularly rich or interesting stratigraphy.

Above Archaeologists take soil samples from the burial site of a Roman stone coffin.

Left These Kubiena tins have been positioned to remove core samples, undisturbed, from different strata, effectively building a picture of how sediments were laid down over time.

Above 'Archaeomagnetic sampling' is often used to date burnt materials, which, upon cooling, retain a magnetization proportional to the direction and intensity of the Earth's magnetic field at that time. Ancient fired objects can thus be dated by comparison with the known record of the Earth's magnetic field.

The significance of age

The age of a site may dictate whether or not there will be a full-time environmentalist on the team and how many samples are taken. We know relatively little about the economies and environments of prehistoric peoples, and some of the big research questions in archaeology specifically concern the development of different forms of agriculture, animal husbandry, horticulture, medicine, food storage, diet, and so on, so all evidence is potentially valuable.

Samples from medieval and post-medieval sites – of which more is known – are taken in quantity only if exceptionally rich deposits are encountered that can help answer specific economic or dietary questions, because there are other sources of data for environmental conditions, including tree-ring data and historical records. The exception to the rule of 'the older the better' are periods for which we have little archaeological data, such as the post-Roman to early medieval period in Europe, because little has survived from what was an organic era, where wood, vegetation, fibre and animal products were the main materials for homes, tools, vessels, transport and religious structures.

Processing Soil Samples

Environmental finds are recovered from bulk and column samples by sieving, or sifting, the soil. This action separates the soil from the larger materials, which are then washed to skim off the lighter materials that will float on the water's surface, making them easier to collect.

Above Small-scale sieving (sifting), of washed samples can be done with a bucket and mesh.

Both bulk and column samples can be processed on the archaeological site, while under the supervision of an environmental archaeologist, or at some later date in a laboratory. In either situation, the techniques for recovering environmental samples are the same – however, the advantage of processing on site is that the feedback is immediate. Deposits that are rich in material can be sampled further and blank samples can be disposed of, saving on effort and storage costs. If samples are not to be processed immediately, they will need storing in an appropriate manner, ideally keeping them in the cold and dark to prevent mould and fungal infection and to ensure that the samples do not dry out.

Flotation

The separation of biological remains from soil works on the principle that the remains are less dense than water, so they will float on the water's surface rather than sinking to the bottom, as do the denser residues. Flotation tanks come in a variety of forms, including versions that constantly recycle the water used in the flotation process, so that they are less wasteful of this precious resource and can be used in situations where the supply of fresh water is limited to what can be brought to the site in containers. Obviously, using water from a pond or stream would be counterproductive because it will contaminate the archaeological samples with modern material.

Whatever form they take, flotation tanks all consist of a mesh that sits on top of a water tank. Soil is placed in the mesh and water is added to the tank so that it rises through the mesh from below. The water has to rise slowly enough for the soil in the mesh to break down and release materials trapped within the lumps and crumbs. The lighter material floats and is carried out of the tank by means of a lip or spillway near the top of the tank. The water that spills over this is then passed through a series of fine sieves (screens) or filters, trapping environmental samples and allowing the water through.

The material caught in the sieves is known as the 'flot', or light fraction, and it consists of plant remains, bone fragments, the smaller and lighter bones of fish, birds, mice, voles or reptiles, insect remains, molluscs and charcoal. The material that is left behind in the floation tank is known as 'heavy fraction', or residue.

Sieving or sifting

Flotation is the technique recommended for capturing smaller and lighter ecofacts, but the heavy fraction might still contain heavier materials, so this is now passed through a series of sieves using running water to help move the soil through the mesh, leaving behind larger particles, including any finds. Sieving – or sifting, as it is also known – can start with a relatively coarse mesh size of 2mm (²⁄₂₅in), which will retrieve charcoal,

Above Screened microscopic finds are suspended in fine mesh bags and left to dry at Çatalhöyük.

Recovering ancient beads

Among the materials that might be missed during excavation but recovered during wet sieving, or wet screening, are the tiny beads that are found in western Asia from the Neolithic period. They are the subject of a research project that is looking at the techniques of early beadmaking at sites that include Wadi Jilat, Jordan, and Çatalhöyük, Turkey, among others.

Analysis involves recovering and studying not just the beads themselves, but also what is known as debitage, the waste flakes and debris that result from bead manufacture. At Çatalhöyük, stone, clay, shell and bone beads have been recovered in quantity from burial sites, and two houses have been identified as possible bead factories on the basis of the quantities of micro-debitage from the obsidian and flint tools that were used to drill holes in the beads.

mollusc shells, small bones and artefacts that might have been hidden in lumps of clay or soil. The remaining soil can then be further sifted, reducing the sieve size each time to 1mm (⅕in), 0.5mm (¹⁄₅₀in) and 0.25mm (¹⁄₁₀₀in). The types of remains trapped at each stage vary: at 1mm/⅕in, the sieve should trap fish scales, eggshell, marine molluscs and bone; reducing the mesh size picks up seeds, pollens and insect remains, which can vary in size from beetle wing cases to microscopic eggs and parasites.

One of the great advantages of wet sieving over dry sieving is that colour contrasts are heightened by water – soil and dust covered artefacts and ecofacts can be easily missed in a dry state but the ivory colour of bone, the black of charcoal, the iridescence of beetle wings or the calcium white of snail shells is far easier to see when water washes away the dust coating.

Breaking up clumps

In both sieving and flotation, some soil lumps will resist being broken down – especially clay. Wet clay that has formed clumps and then been baked for weeks by high temperatures and hot sun is difficult to break up. In this case, prior to processing, samples of dry material can be soaked in a solution of hydrogen peroxide, using protective gloves. A less effective dispersant that must be used with samples from waterlogged remains is the water softener known as Calgon (sodium hexametaphosphate, or amorphous sodium polyphospate), which, unlike hydrogen peroxide, does not harm plant remains.

Storage

Material collected by both processes of sieving and flotation is usually laid out to dry. Care must be taken to ensure that any light material does not blow away if being dried outdoors. The dry materials are then bagged and labelled. Any plant remains from waterlogged sites are the exception. The residue from these samples is placed in a jar and covered with water.

Wet sieving finds

1 Water is used in wet sieving to break up larger lumps of soil and find the very small objects that might be hidden inside.

2 First the soil from the area being sampled is mixed with water to break down the clods and make a runny mud mixture.

3 The resulting mud is then poured through a series of sieves with a finer and finer mesh, leaving a residue in each sieve.

4 This is messy work, and it is often necessary to break up stubborn lumps by hand to make sure all the soil passes through the mesh.

5 Each of the sieves is then laid out in the sunshine to dry; at this stage the contents consist of a mix of stones and small finds.

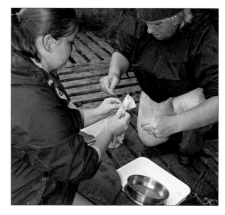

6 Once dry, the residue is bagged and labelled for lab analysis; the final stage is to pick out finds, such as seeds, bones and beads.

The Study of Human Remains

Human remains can tell archaeologists an enormous amount about past lives and cultures. The many beliefs that people have about the sanctity of the grave, which affected how they were buried, give an insight into their cultures – and the bones themselves provide archaeological information.

Above Strong beliefs about life and death mean human remains must be treated with care.

It is precisely because so many different beliefs surround the treatment of the dead that human remains are of such importance to archaeologists. Respect for the dead is a fundamental trait that defines the human species and distinguishes us from most of our closest cousins in the evolutionary tree. Much of what archaeologists know about the very early development of human characteristics comes from burials.

Body and soul

People have in the past treated the deceased in an extraordinary variety of ways that give us glimpses of their beliefs. Some expose their dead, believing that the birds that feed on flesh carry the soul to heaven (archaeologists call this 'excarnation'); others bury the dead with a variety of gifts and possessions ('articulated' or 'extended' burial), while others bind up the dead using cloth or cord so that they resemble a foetus in the womb ('flexed' or 'crouch' burials), perhaps placing them in a stone-lined chamber ('cist' burial), while others again practise cremation and bury the ashes in a specially made urn, or scatter them on the surface of a river.

Some religions believe that body and soul are indivisible, and that to disturb the dead is to cause them distress; others believe that only the soul survives after death, and that the physical body is unimportant – in medieval Europe bodies were routinely dug up after a period of time and the bones stored in charnel houses, making room for new graves. By contrast, some cultures practised ritual embalming or mummification – the ancient Egyptians preserved humans, birds and animals in this way, as did the Christian Church during the Middle Ages, to preserve the bodies of saints, and more

Below Mummified human remains uncovered in the Egyptian desert are covered with a protective mesh.

recently, the Soviet Union afforded the same treatment to its leader Vladimir Lenin (1870–1924).

From studying prehistoric burial practice, archaeologists also think that some people believed in a third transitional state between life and death. Archaeological evidence suggest that some people in the past stored the remains of their dead relatives for a year or more, before taking them to large ritual gatherings where the 'half-dead' were ritually reunited with their ancestors, after which the physical remains were discarded by being placed in pits, burned or placed on rafts and sent down rivers. Other cultures place an entirely different value on the human remains. In southern Asia, people visit the graves of their ancestors several times a year, clean the grave, polish the bones and put out food, money and gifts for the dead.

The value of human remains

Apart from the value to archaeologists of human remains as a cultural indicator, providing details about the lifestyles and beliefs of the community whose dead are being studied, the remains themselves can tell us much about life in the past. Scientific analysis of human remains can tell archaeologists about the age of the deceased, their diet, their state of health and any diseases, injuries or chronic conditions they suffered from, what sort of lifestyle they led – sedentary or active, for example – and whether they show evidence of battle wounds or hunting injuries. Adding all this data together brings a wealth of information about populations and communities – whether the people of a Roman town, a medieval village, the monks of a monastic community, the victims of a plague or epidemic, or the dead of a defeated army.

In recent years, even more exciting developments in the study of genetic material from human remains is opening up new lines of research about human origins and the migration of peoples to all parts of the globe. We are

Above Recovering graves from the 1st–3rd centuries AD in Beirut, Libya.

Science needs human remains

Archaeologists treat the excavation of human remains as an opportunity to learn about the past. However, they now excavate according to codes of practice that have been developed in consultation with governments and communities to avoid causing offence or transgressing community rights and beliefs. As a general rule, human remains are usually excavated because they are found accidentally or because they are under threat anyway from development or natural erosion. In one case, a parish church wanted to extend its graveyard into an adjoining field. Imagine the surprise of the local community when archaeologists checked the field for remains and found that it was already a cemetery – filled with the remains of the people who had lived in the same parish 1,500 years ago.

Above One of the tombs of the Merowe site in Sudan, where the remains of ancient Kushan rulers from 250BC–AD300 are housed in spectacular fashion.

Above A mummified body is excavated at the Bahariya oasis, Egypt, a site rich in Romano–Egyptian human remains and dubbed 'The Valley of the Golden Mummies'.

beginning at last to be able to answer some of the really big questions in archaeology. For example, do humans have a single point of origin (Africa) or did humans evolve independently in different parts of the world (including China, Russia and Indonesia)? When did humans arrive in America and from where? Did the transition from a nomadic hunting and gathering existence to a more settled agricultural lifestyle spread because people

migrated and took domesticated seeds and animals with them, or because the idea of agriculture spread rapidly, without any human migration? Similarly, how many of the great seismic changes in society have occurred because people have imposed those ideas on a society that they have invaded, defeated or colonized, and how much are they due to the fact that good ideas, like fashion trends, are rapidly adopted by everybody?

Human Remains: Legal and Ethical Issues

Finding human remains during an excavation can open up all types of legal and ethical issues, which archaeologists need to be aware of before they excavate. In some cultures, there is a need to honour the dead and ensure that their spirits remain at peace by not disturbing their graves.

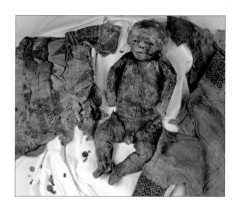

Above The 13th-century remains of this infant, found in Lebanon, testify to mummification skills.

The laws relating to the discovery of human remains vary from country to country, but usually the site director is required to inform a civil authority, such as a coroner, when a grave or burial is found. The coroner will consider the evidence and decide whether or not a forensic investigation is needed. If the archaeological evidence points to this being an ancient burial, and not a more recent crime, permission will be given, usually as a written licence, to enable the remains to be excavated – to do so before the licence is issued might be illegal.

The issuing of a licence doesn't mean that the remains will be dug up. As a rule, archaeologists try not to disturb human remains. They will only do so if the remains are to be destroyed anyway – for example, because the site is to be developed – or because the potential scientific value of studying the remains is judged to outweigh the importance of leaving the human remains at rest.

Links with the past

As well as having a general duty to ensure that all human remains are treated with respect and dignity,

archaeologists have a specific duty to take into account the views of living descendants, whose views are accorded considerable weight in any discussions concerning the excavation and treatment of remains.

The need to consult descendants can occur where a cemetery is excavated that contains relatively recent burials. This happened in London, where the route of the Channel Tunnel Rail Link passed through the site of the churchyard of St Pancras Church. The decision to route the rail link through the cemetery was controversial and was not one that archaeologists supported, however, once planners and engineers decided to go ahead, archaeologists used parish burial registers and coffin labels to identify as many of the dead as possible so that relatives could be

Below Twelve skeletons discovered in 2004 at the Azetc Teotihuacan site, near Mexico City, are believed to be the remains of warriors who were captured and sacrificed in around AD 200–250.

Below This mummified hand is part of a headless mummy that was excavated in Lima, Peru, in 2005. The mummy is believed to have belonged to the Wari culture, and date back some 4,000 years.

Right A more or less complete skeleton, some 4,000 years old, is recovered at Ikiztepe, Turkey.

consulted about reburial arrangements. Many of the graves identified turned out to be French aristocrats who had fled the French Revolution, which began in 1789, including the Archbishop of Narbonne and Primate of Languedoc.

Indigenous people

As well as specific named relatives, the definition of descendants might also include a broad class of people, as is the case in the Americas, Canada and Australia, where First Nations, or indigenous people, have to be consulted by law when ancient human remains are discovered. In the United States, the Native American Graves Protection and Repatriation Act specifically prohibits the excavation of sites likely to contain human remains, funerary or sacred objects, or items of cultural and religious importance to Native American or Native Hawaiian people. The law extends to any other ethnic group or community that historically ascribes cultural or symbolic value to the site and might object to the site's excavation.

Reburial

One area of public debate surrounding the study of human remains is the question of reburial once scientific laboratory work as been completed. The Anglican Church advocates reburial, unless there is 'significant future research potential', in which case they argue for the storage of human remains in a suitable holding institution, such as a disused church. In the United Kingdom, the archaeologists who excavated the disused Anglo Saxon church of St Peter, Barton upon Humber, North Lincolnshire, have now built a specially designed chapel to house the remains of the 3,000 individuals exhumed during the excavation. The excavated remains can rest on consecrated ground, but are still accessible to researchers.

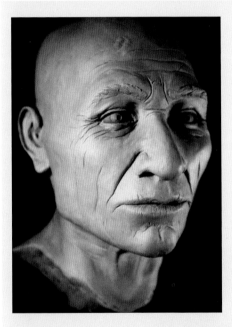

Above An interpretation of how Kennewick Man might have looked, reconstructed from remains found on a river bank in 1996.

Kennewick Man

One celebrated example of a discovery that has tested the United States' laws on the treatment of human remains is the case of 'Kennewick Man'. The bones of Kennewick Man were found in 1996, emerging from an eroded river bank along a stretch of the Columbia River near Kennewick, Washington, by an archaeologist called Jim Chatters, who had been systematically studying the river's archaeology over a period of time. The sediments in which the bones were found suggested that the remains were unusually ancient – and scientific tests later indicated that Kennewick man had died at the age of 40 in around 8000BC.

The date places Kennewick Man as an early settler in North America, but archaeologists were hampered from further study by a law requiring them to hand the remains over to American First Nation groups for reburial. Chatters appealed against the law, and, after ten years of legal process, won the right to conduct further scientific tests. He argued from the skeletal evidence and the skull shape that Kennewick Man was descended from an entirely different group of migrants from those that account for today's First Nation people, and that they were not, therefore, his descendants. He also argued that the universal value of the information likely to be gained from studying Kennewick Man outweighed First Nation religious sensitivities.

Human Remains: Excavation Techniques

Some sites are known in advance to be cemeteries or graveyards. However, human remains can also turn up in some unexpected places, so all archaeologists have to be aware of the relevant codes of practice and the correct excavation procedures.

Above A dental pick is being used to remove soil around human vertebrae.

Taking into account religious and ethical issues, public attitudes, and the value and benefit of scientific study, archaeologists try to ensure that the work of excavating and removing human remains is not visible to the general public. This is not a concern on excavations where the public are not permitted and cannot see the site, but in publicly accessible areas, the site might be screened off or the grave area screened with a tent.

Health and safety

The health of the archaeologists working with human remains is also considered, and they might need to wear protective clothing. This is true when working with recent human remains, especially those buried in airtight coffins where soft tissue can survive – and with it the threat of disease – or, in the case of lead coffins, which can cause lead poisoning.

Archaeologists working on the excavation of a church crypt in London, for example, were glad that they had taken the necessary precautions to avoid contact with disease. Some of the skeletons they found were diagnosed, from characteristic lesions around the knees, to have died from smallpox, a dangerous and highly contagious disease. Another advantage of wearing protective clothing and breathing equipment in such circumstances is that they protect the remains themselves from contamination, which is important if ancient DNA material is to be recovered.

Excavation considerations

The strategy for recovering the human remains and any associated artefacts will depend on the nature of the site, the state of preservation and the likely knowledge to be gained by excavation. One basic decision is if the remains should be excavated on site or block-lifted by cutting around and under the remains. This preserves the surrounding soil so that the coffin, cremation urn or grave contents can be excavated under laboratory conditions.

This was done, for example, in the case of a Roman lead coffin found in London in 1999, which was brought to the Museum of London for opening, an event witnessed by TV cameras. Among the finds that might have been lost under less controlled conditions

Above During the famous excavation of the 'Spanish lady of Spitalfields' by archaeologists in London, broadcast live on television, the threat of active 'plague' bacteria required full protective gear to be worn.

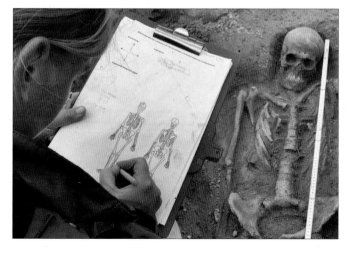

Above These human remains, which are being measured and recorded, were excavated at a 13th-century village – part of a rescue project preceding extension of Berlin's Schoenfeld Airport, Germany.

Lifting and packaging human remains

Recent research at Bristol University, England, has perfected luminescence techniques for dating human remains by measuring the decay of various elements in the bone, and in the quartz of sand in the surrounding soil.

1 Rather than clean the remains on site, skulls are lifted using gloves to prevent contamination from modern matter.

2 The intact skull is potentially full of information about dates, diet and possible injuries.

Above Volcano victims from Pompeii are displayed to museum visitors in Italy.

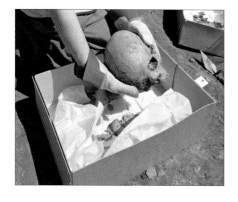

3 The skull is carefully packed in acid-free tissue paper to prevent damage during transit to the laboratory.

were leaves and flowers placed in the coffin as a funeral garland, along with the remains of a glass flask, which probably held perfumed ointments.

Recording the excavation

Unless there are reasons for preserving the find intact, it is more normal to record the grave through photography and written records. These will note key diagnostic details about the burial practice, such as the orientation (which way the head and feet are facing in relation to the compass points), and whether the skeleton is laid out fully extended or crouched, flexed (with the knees up against the chest and hands

near the chin), or supine (face upward, lying on the back) or prone (on the front, face downward).

Rather than drawing the skeleton, which requires a good knowledge of human anatomy, pre-printed skeleton diagrams can be used to record features of the burial, such as the position of arms, hands, legs and feet, any visible grave goods, the condition of the bone, any missing parts, any parts in unusual positions, any disturbances to the burial, and, of course, the stratigraphical relationships of the grave to any other archaeological features. However, pre-printed sheets are of no use when dealing with multiple burials, or with animal remains, so the excavation and recording of human remains is normally entrusted to someone with a good knowledge of anatomy.

Experienced staff can often excavate, record and lift a skeleton in half a day. They will systematically place the bones in labelled plastic bags according to the body's anatomy, so that the skull, torso, legs and arms are lifted and bagged up separately, with hand and foot bones being bagged with the corresponding leg or arm bones. Soil samples will also be taken to recover small artefacts or biological remains. Particular attention is given to the abdominal, chest and

What does the public think?

In 2005, researchers at Cambridge University, England, carried out a survey to find out what members of the public thought about the excavation of human remains and their display in museums. The result was that 88 per cent believed it was appropriate for human remains to be used for scientific study. More than 70 per cent felt that eventual reburial was desirable, but only when such studies were completed. Only 5 per cent wanted immediate reburial.

The views of archaeologists and the general public seem to be broadly in line, but there are some areas where there was a surprising degree of divergence. Of those questioned, 56 per cent believed that the assumed religion of the deceased should affect how the skeleton was reburied, despite the fact that we cannot know with any certainty what our prehistoric ancestors believed. This raises the difficult question of who, if anyone, has the right to speak for prehistoric people? Is it right to use neo-Pagan or Christian burial rites for people whose religious practices can only be guessed at?

head areas of the body to retrieve evidence of gallstones, food remains or parasites.

Case Study: the Prittlewell Prince

A well-preserved and unrobbed 7th-century burial chamber – packed with the possessions of the deceased – was excavated at Priory Crescent, Prittlewell, Essex, in the south-east of England, in the autumn of 2003. The sheer quality of the finds was outstanding.

Above A gold belt buckle, one of the princely treasures found at Prittlewell, being excavated.

The excavation of this site was special not only for the quality of the finds, but also because the archaeological team displayed an enormous amount of skill in extracting the maximum amount of information from a site that consisted of little but sand. The site was found by a team from the Museum of London Archaeology Service (MoLAS) on a piece of land that was due to be destroyed by a road widening scheme.

Before excavation began, the team used desktop research to establish that Anglo-Saxon graves had been found on the site on three previous occasions: in the 1880s, during the building of the London to Southend railway line; in 1923, when the houses of Priory Crescent were built; and in 1930, when workmen noticed the remains of Saxon and Roman burials in the railway cutting. The objects found in these graves suggested that the cemetery was in use between AD500 and AD700.

A vanished tomb

Nothing, however, suggested the likely burial of a man of power and wealth, which is what the MoLAS team found in 2003. At the south end of the site, where archaeologists were trowelling over the sandy subsoil, they found a rectangular area of soil, subtly different in colour from the surrounding soil.

After three months of painstaking excavation, the MoLAS team were able to reveal that this was the site of an intact and undisturbed chamber grave, measuring 4m (13ft) long and wide, and 1.5m (5ft) deep. The chamber had been dug and then lined with wooden planks, to resemble the appearance of a timber hall. A roof of timber covered the grave, which was then covered by a large burial mound, in typical Anglo-Saxon fashion.

Over time, the timber roof of the buried chamber began to rot and sand slowly trickled through and into the hollow chamber beneath, eventually filling the chamber to the brim. The high acidity of the sand filling in the chamber meant that organic materials, including the body, did not survive – however, they had left their imprint in the form of slight staining in the Essex sand.

With remarkable precision, the sand was excavated to reveal not only the outline of the bed on which the deceased was laid upon the chamber floor, but also the remains of his possessions. These had remained in their original positions, pinned in place

Left and above The bronze bowl is typical of styles known from eastern England in the 7th century. By contrast, a bronze flagon (drinking vessel) from the same period, bearing embossed medallions (see opposite page, top right), was almost certainly a Mediterranean import.

Above This 'folding stool' probably originated from territory in modern-day Slovakia, which was at that time part of Lombardic Italy.

by the sand from the mound above. Because of the fragility of the finds, many of them were lifted from the grave in blocks of soil for excavation in the laboratory. By utilizing this technique, archaeologists doubled the number of finds initially recovered from the site from 60 to 120.

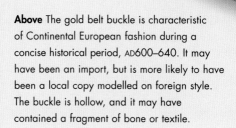

Above The gold belt buckle is characteristic of Continental European fashion during a concise historical period, AD600–640. It may have been an import, but is more likely to have been a local copy modelled on foreign style. The buckle is hollow, and it may have contained a fragment of bone or textile.

Treasured possessions

The finds included a sword and shoe buckles found at the side and foot of the coffin bed. Bronze cauldrons and flagons were found hanging from iron nails hammered into the walls of the house-like tomb, and equipment for feasting was carefully arranged around the body, including glass bowls from Asia Minor, a Byzantine flagon, decorated hanging bowls from Ireland, buckets and drinking horns with gilded mounts. Valued personal possessions laid with the deceased included a gaming board, folded textiles, a solid gold belt buckle, gold coins from Merovingian France, a sword and shield, and a lyre and a folding throne of Italian design.

Most tellingly, a pair of small, gold-foil crosses were found on the body, indicating that the tomb's occupant might have been a Christian, and this combination of pagan burial practice (furnishing the deceased with goods for use in the next world) and Christian symbol held the clues to the possible identity of the deceased.

Identifying the deceased

From historical records we know that St Augustine of Canterbury was sent to England in AD596 by Pope Gregory the Great with the task of converting the Anglo-Saxon tribes to Christianity. There are records of two East Saxon kings who adopted Christianity: King Saebert, who died in AD616, and his grandson, Sigebert II, who was murdered in 653.

Possibly, this could be the grave of either Saebert or Sigebehrt, although neither name fits with the name found on a silver spoon recovered from the tomb. It was engraved with two worn and incomplete inscriptions, one of which reads 'FAB...' and the other 'RONAM...'. Perhaps the inscriptions on the spoon form part of the new name that one of these two kings chose as a Christian name when being baptized.

Above Each of the three embossed medallions on the cast bronze flagon shows a figure, thought to be a saint on horseback – in a style that suggests Mediterranean origins.

Other discoveries made in the Museum of London laboratory include a set of 57 plain bone pieces and two large deer-antler dice from some kind of game, as well as a lyre, which is being described as the most complete lyre of the period yet seen in Britain. These artefacts have prompted the popular press to speculate that 'the Prince of Prittlewell', a high-ranking aristocrat who lived in Essex 1,400 years ago, was not only a Christian, but was also fond of music and board games.

Below Two gold foil crosses were among the most significant of the finds in the burial chamber. Of Latin origin, they suggest a strong allegiance to Christianity and are likely to have been grave goods customized specially for the burial ceremony.

Timeline

This timeline presents a selective list of significant milestones and events in the history of places and civilizations featured in this book.

7 million years ago	**Africa**	Our oldest known ancestor: *Sahelanthropus tchadensis*, found in northern Chad in 2002.
3.2 million years ago	**Africa**	'Lucy' (*Australopithecus afarensis*) found in Ethiopia's Awash Valley in 1974.
2.5 million years ago	**Africa**	The first stone tools.
1.5 million years ago	**Africa**	The earliest evidence for controlled fire use from fossil hearths and burnt animal bones from sites in Kenya and from the Swartkrans Cave in South Africa.
800,000 years ago	**Africa**	Archaic hominins begin to spread from East Africa as part of the first 'out of Africa' wave of migration.
500,000 years ago	**Far East**	'Peking Man', *Homo erectus pekinensis*, is found at Zhoukoudian, near Beijing (Peking) in 1923, cousin to the 'Java Man' *Homo erectus* remains found in Indonesia in 1891.
300,000 years ago	**Africa**	The first evidence of body art: stone tools from Zambia used for the grinding of pigments.
150,000 to 130,000 years ago	**Africa**	Modern humans (*Homo sapiens*) evolve as a new species in eastern or southern Africa.
100,000 years ago	**Africa**	*Homo sapiens* begins to migrate out of Africa into Asia and Europe. Shell beads of this date found in Israel and Algeria.
73,000 years ago	**Africa**	The first known art: an ochre block marked with an abstract design from South Africa's Blombos Cave.
50,000 years ago	**Australia**	The first *Homo sapiens* reach Australia; stone tools from Lake Mungo and rock art at Dampier.
41,000 years ago	**Europe**	Oldest known musical instrument: bone flute made by *H. neanderthlenisis*.
35,000 years ago	**America**	The date when geneticists believe the first humans might have arrived in America, though there is no undisputed physical evidence for this.
23,000 years ago	**Africa and Europe**	Seeking refuge in caves around the Mediterranean and Atlantic coasts, modern humans manage to survive successive ice ages, while Neanderthals succumb to cold and hunger.
20,000 years ago	**Europe, Asia and the Americas**	The Mesolithic: a transitional period during which the climate begins to warm after the last ice age; today's seas, rivers and coastlines begin to form and islands are created that separate people from each other so they begin to evolve new languages and cultures.
18,000 years ago	**Americas**	The probable date at which humans arrived in America across the frozen Bering Straits from Siberia. Later migrants arrived some 13,000 years ago by boat from Japan.
11,000 years ago	**Asia, spreading to Europe**	The Neolithic: the beginnings of agriculture, pottery and permanent settlement.
4800BC	**Asia**	Copper tools from Mehrgarh, in modern Pakistan, indicate early metal-working on an industrial scale.
4000BC	**Asia**	Bronze tools are made in Harappa, Pakistan, and the technology spreads to Iran and Iraq by 3500BC and from there to the Aegean.
3800BC	**Europe**	The first long barrows and ceremonial enclosures are built in Europe, land cleared and farmed.

3500BC	**Asia**	The first written records in the form of cuneiform clay tablets from lower Mesopotamia (modern Iraq). The first city states with a priestly governor or king, living in a temple/palace.
3300BC	**Europe**	Death of 'Ötzi the Iceman', aged about 45, on the modern border between Austria and Italy, carrying a flint knife and copper axe.
3100BC	**Europe**	Henge monuments, such as Stonehenge, Woodhenge and Durrington Walls, suggest astronomical knowledge and large winter solstice gatherings.
2700BC	**Europe**	Minoan civilization on the Aegean island of Crete based on large palaces with central control over food and other resources.
2650BC	**Africa and Asia**	The Great Pyramid of Khufu, Egypt's first pyramid. Wheeled sledges and bullock carts in India
2600BC	**Asia**	Planned towns in the Indus Valley, Pakistan, with piped water and drains. Wheel-made pottery invented in China.
2000BC	**Asia**	Abraham, the father of the Jewish people, is thought to have lived around this time; the Exodus of the Jewish people from Egypt to the Promised Land probably took place between 1444 and 1290BC.
1800BC	**Europe and Asia**	Early iron-working in Asia, but iron only supplants bronze when tin supplies are disrupted from about 1200BC.
1500BC	**Asia Pacific**	The Lapita people, boat-borne migrants from Taiwan, Vietnam and the Philippines, begin to colonize the islands of the Pacific.
1200BC	**Americas**	First Mayan cities and ceremonial centres established along the coast of Mexico.
1194BC	**Europe**	Probable date of the events described in Homer's *Iliad*, based on burnt layers at the city of Troy.
800BC	**Europe**	The Iron Age in Europe (characterized by Celtic metalwork), which ends as Rome begins to expand and develop its empire from 340BC.
776BC	**Europe**	Olympic Games established at the sanctuary of Zeus, in the ancient Greek city of Olympia.
AD1–100	**Mediterranean**	• 64 Nero constructs the Domus Aurea after a fire in Rome. • 79 Mount Vesuvius erupts destroying Pompeii and Herculaneum.
	Americas	The Moche culture emerges in coastal northern Peru.
AD500	**Americas**	The Central Mexican city of Teotihuacán reaches its height in the 6th century. The burial mounds at Sutton Hoo are in use from the late 6th century.
AD600	**Europe**	The Ancestral Puebloan (Anasazi) Indian society flourishes in Mesa Verde.
AD800	**Americas**	Occupation begins at the Mayan city of Chichén Itzá.
AD1000	**Americas**	A group of Scandinavians settle at L'Anse aux Meadows in Newfoundland.
AD1350	**Oceania**	Shag River Mouth in New Zealand is occupied for about 50 years.
AD1400	**Americas**	The Chimú are conquered by the Incas and the assimilation of their culture greatly influences the course of Inca civilization.
AD1492	**Americas**	The first voyage of Columbus is taken as the start of the modern era in archaeology and history, and the beginning of the process of globalization.
AD1700	**Oceania**	HMS *Pandora* sinks in Australia's Great Barrier Reef in the 1790s.
AD1800	**Americas**	1876 The Battle of Little Bighorn takes place.

Index

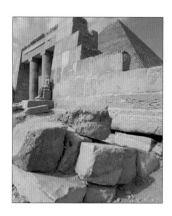

PICTURE CREDITS

(b: bottom, l: left, m: middle, r: right, t: top). Anness Publishing Ltd would like to thank the following people for location photography: **Wiggold Summer School,** Abbey Home Farm, Cirencester, UK, to Will and Hilary Chester-Master at Abbey Home Farm and Professor Timothy Darvill at the School of Conservation Sciences, University of Bournemouth, UK, and **Berkeley Castle Summer School,** Gloucestershire, UK, to Dr Stuart Prior and Dr Mark Horton of the Department of Archaeology and Anthropology, University of Bristol, UK, in conjunction with the Berkeley Castle Charitable Trust, for permission to photograph. Thanks also to the students of the School of Conservation Sciences and those who attended the summer school; **Bristol Harbourside Excavation,** thanks to Jim Dyer of

Crest Nicholson South West Ltd, Bristol, for permission to photograph the excavation, and to the employees of Wessex Archaeology for featuring in the photographs. The following photographs are ©**Anness Publishing Ltd** 9b, 32t, 35r, 38t, 39tl, 39tr, 39ml, 39mr, 40t, 41b, 50bl, 50br, 50mr, 52t, 53bl, 53br, 53mr, 56, 57m, 63t, 64b, 65t, 66bl, 69bm, 69bl, 70br, 71t, 72t, 72br, 72bl, 73b, 77t, 77b, 79tl, 80t, 81tl, 81tr, 81ml, 81mr, 82b, 83tl, 84br, 84bl, 85tl, 85tm, 86t, 87b, 89tr, 89tl, 89b, 93b, 94t, 94b, 95tl, 95tm, 95tr, 95bl, 95bm, 95br, 97r, 101tl, 100tr, 100bl, 100br, 102t, 102bl, 102br, 106bl, 111tl, 111b, 115tr, 115tl, 115mr, 115ml, 115br, 115bl, 120t, 121tl, 121tm, 121b **Alamy** 23b **Amsterdam University Library, Special Collections** 17t, 17b **Anthony Duke ©Anness Publishing Ltd** 24b, 45b, 48bl, 48bm, 48br, 70m, 70bl, 87tl, 87tm, 87tr, 93tr **Antiquity Publications Ltd** 25t **Archaeological Computing Laboratory, University of Sydney** /Andrew Wilson 18t, 26t, 26b, 27tr /Damian Evans 27tl, 27bl, 27br **The Berkeley Castle Charitable Trust** 5b, 30b **Berkeley Historic Maps and Images, University of Bristol** 30ml, 30mr **Çatalhöyük Research Project** 97m, 108t, 114b **Charlene Brown** 5t, 40b **Christopher Catling** 19mr, 36b

Corbis 3t, 6t, 7t, 7b, 8br, 10, 13bl, 14b, 15b, 22t, 28t, 29b, 37t, 37b, 39b, 47tr, 68b, 71b, 75t, 90br, 97l, 98t, 98b, 105tr, 105b, 118t **The Cultural Resources Program, Fort Bragg** 106br **Dale Croes** 99t, 99ml, 99mr **Dominic Powlesland, Landscape Research Centre** 49 **Dries Dossche** 62t **Erica Utsi** 51t **Fiona Haughey** 62b, 76t, 84t, 88b **The Flag Fen Bronze Age Centre** /John Byford and Mike Webber 105tl **Gareth Beale, Archaeological Computing Research Group, University of Southampton** 54t, 55b **Getty Images** 6b, 12b, 15t, 21b, 22b, 33b, 47tl, 61b, 67b, 74bl, 80b, 86b, 96, 100t, 116b, 117br, 117bl, 117t, 118bl, 118br, 119t, 119b, 120br, 121tr **Gloucestershire Archives** 19ml **Gloucester City Museums** 19t **GUARD, Glasgow University** 68t, 110br, 113tl **Guildhall Library, City of London** 13t ©**iStockphoto.com** 3b, 41tl, Björn Kindler 20t /Clifford Shirley 11r /Darren Hendley 16t /Lukasz Laska 41tr /Rich Legg 43br /Steven Allan 18b /Wolfgang Feischl 52b **Katharina Neumann** 107b **Lucy Doncaster** 20b **Macphail, R. I. and Crowther, J. 2004** 109r **Margot Mulcahy** 21t **Martin Millet** 91t **Musuem of London Archaeology Service** 83bl, 90bl, 107tr, 111tr, 112br, 120bl /Andy Chopping 59b, 99bl, 108br, 110t,

122bl, 123tl, 123tr, 123bl, 123br /Maggie Cox 103b, 103t, 109l, 113b, 122t /Trevor Hurst 107tl **Natasha Mulder** 19b **The Ordnance Survey** (reproduced from 1909 Ordnance Survey map) 16bl **The Oxford Archaeological Unit Ltd** 8l, 9t, 11m, 13br, 14t, 38b, 43bl, 44b, 53t, 58b, 60b, 63b, 64t, 65b, 66t, 69br, 74br, 78b, 82t, 88t, 90t, 91b, 92t, 92b, 104t, 108bl, 116t **Pietro Laureano, 2005** 28m, 28bl, 28br **Professor Simon Keay, British School at Rome/ Graeme Earl, University of Southampton** 54b, 54m, 55t, 55ml, 55mr **Professor T Darvill, University of Bournemouth** 32b **Science Photo Library** 46bl **Sheffield City Archives** 16ml, 16mr **Tehmina Goskar** 30t **Wessex Archaeology** 8bl, 33t, 34, 35m, 35l, 36t, 40m, 42t, 42b, 45t, 46t, 46br, 48t, 50t, 51bl, 51br, 57l, 57r, 58t, 59t, 60t, 61mr, 61t, 61ml, 66m, 66br, 67t, 70t, 73t, 75b, 76b, 78t, 79tr, 79b, 81b, 83br, 83tr, 85tr, 99br, 106t, 110bl, 112bl, 112t, 113tr, 114t **University of Reading** 101b **Vance McCollum, South Carolina State Museum** 104b **www.lastrefuge.co.uk** / Adrian Warren 23t 24t /Dae Sasitorn 11l, 25b, 74t **www.webbaviation.co.uk** 16br

Hickmans

Brunswick County Library
109 W Moore Street
Southport, NC 28461

WITHDRAWN